H. M. Prison.
Reading.

waiting I have determined to
you sake as for mine, as I
as passed through two long
es having received a single line
ven, except such as gave me

le friendship has ended in ruin
te memory & our ancient affection
rt loathing, ~~bitterness~~ and contempt
Heart once held by love is very
e, I think, best in your heart
the loneliness & prison-life
without my permission or
though the world will know
or passion, of remorse or
ed as your answer or your

April 2000.

Dear Margot,

This keepsake will Remind
you of a most extraodinary
evening of pure theatre
at the Gate.

Anne

THE
WILDE ALBUM

THE
WILDE ALBUM

Merlin Holland

FOURTH ESTATE • *London*

Acknowledgements

Apart from the help I received from the staff of some of the lending institutions, I am particularly grateful to the following: Davis Coakley, Mary Lady Eccles, Owen Dudley Edwards, Herb Gstalder, Sir Rupert Hart-Davis, Jeremy Mason, Joy Melville, Michael Meredith, Daniel Novak, Ulick O'Connor, Julia Rosenthal, Nicholas Scheetz, Steve Tabor, Peter Vernier, Francis Wyndham. Collectors, friends or fellow searchers in the Wildean labyrinth, I am more indebted to them than space will allow me to express individually. Christopher Potter at Fourth Estate and Robert Updegraff who designed the book let me participate in its creation which was an unexpected pleasure and a privilege.

First published in Great Britain in 1997 by
Fourth Estate Limited
6 Salem Road
London W2 4BU

Copyright © 1997 by Merlin Holland

3 5 7 9 10 8 6 4 2

The right of Merlin Holland to be identified as the author of this work has been asserted by him in accordance with the Copyright, Designs and Patents Act 1988.

A catalogue record for this book is available from the British Library.

ISBN 1-85702-782-5

Designed by Robert Updegraff

Printed in Great Britain by Hillman Printers (Frome) Limited, Somerset

Half-title page **Oscar Wilde, seen by Max Beerbohm. Many of Beerbohm's cartoons of Wilde were drawn after his death and dated so; this is undated and so undatable but represents him at his most corpulent around 1893.**
Title page **Wilde photographed by Napoleon Sarony in New York at the start of his lecture tour of the US in 1882. No 23 in the numbered series.**

Introduction

The Wilde family album . . . if only it had been so simple. Oh, it existed
– three of them in fact – alongside the three volumes of press cuttings,
caricatures of him and parodies of his work: you would have expected
no less from the master self-publicist. The sheriff's men sold all six for
twenty-five shillings along with everything else in his Tite Street home
the day before the Crown took him to court the first time. Twenty years
of that brilliant, outrageous life in which he had dared to challenge the
smug hypocrisy of his age, were torn symbolically from him by the Law.
I imagine it must have hurt Oscar almost as much as losing all his
presentation copies and fine bindings.

But the dispersal of those volumes is part of our family story. It had
to be so; there was something Greek and inevitable about his downfall,
and from it has come an extraordinary voyage of discovery for me
lasting thirty years, finding the grandfather I never knew, first through
words and now through images. In the caricatures you glimpse a little of
how his contemporaries saw him; in the studio photographs something
of the way he wanted the world to see him; and I hope, like me, you are
able to hear faint echoes of that voice 'the texture of brown velvet and
played like a cello' in the quotes from his letters.

Merlin Holland
LONDON, 1997

The Ireland into which my grandfather was born in the mid-1850s was a deeply scarred nation. A million of its people had died in the famine years from 1845 to 1849 and another million and a half had emigrated in an attempt to escape the horrors of starvation, though many of those in turn had died of fever and malnutrition on the way. Anti-English feeling was running high since the Anglo-Irish landowners, while obviously not responsible for the potato blight, somehow became guilty by association with the callous *laissez-faire* policies of Westminster and certainly made matters no easier for themselves by exporting more grain than ever to England from the bumper harvest of 1846. In the midst of all this, in 1847, Daniel O'Connell died. The first Irish Catholic MP, he had founded a movement to repeal the Act of Union, which became a focal point for the growing Anglophobia. Without its leader, but more obviously because of the main priority of its grassroots supporters was now finding enough food for the body and not just for the soul, the movement fizzled out. The final blow to the movement came in 1848 when a militant splinter group called the Young Irelanders was dispersed after their failed 'Rising' at Ballingarry, in truth a farcical skirmish with the police, better known as 'the battle of Widow MacCormack's cabbage garden'. Ireland lay down for a while to lick its wounds.

Above **Oscar Wilde at eight** *(Photo Metropolitan Photo Co., Dublin)*

Opposite **Oscar Wilde, aged about ten; a crayon drawing by an unknown artist.**

What possible relevance, you may wonder, does any of this have to the Oscar Wilde whom we have come to know as the urbane London dandy, the master of the epigrammatic riposte and the author of one of the most enduring social comedies in the English language, *The Importance of Being Earnest*? The stark contrast between post-famine Ireland and the glitter of 1890s London with which we invariably associate him, could scarcely be greater and yet the imprint of those early years on the young Wilde, in particular the influence of his two remarkable parents, strongly committed Hibernophiles both, he intellectually and she more emotionally, was to remain with him throughout his life. He may, as he says, have lost his Dublin accent soon after arriving at Oxford as an undergraduate, since it would have separated him linguistically from his contemporaries, perhaps even caused him embarrassment, but later his Irishness would set him apart from what he regarded as the commonplace in English life and letters and was more a matter in which to take pride. 'We Irish are too poetical to be poets,' W. B. Yeats recalls him saying around 1888. 'We are a nation of brilliant failures but we are the greatest talkers since the Greeks.' To be Irish was to be subversive but above all it was to be imaginative, qualities rooted deep in his nation's culture and history and which, at the same time as they marked both the author and the man as an individual in an age of conformity, also wrote his name clearly into the lists of public undesirables. 'My cradle was rocked by the Fates,' he wrote to his friend Carlos Blacker in 1897, but the hand had a strangely Celtic feel to it.

William Wilde, Oscar's father, was a doctor and the son of a doctor, Thomas, who had practised at Castlereagh, County Roscommon in the early years of the nineteenth century. Thomas christened his son William Robert Wills in deference to a close friend and wealthy local landowner of the same name; the Wills element of his name would in turn be passed on to Oscar. By the time he was twenty-eight William Wilde had graduated as a doctor, completed a voyage to Madeira, Teneriffe, North Africa and the Middle East, studied at Moorfields Eye Hospital in London and spent time with some of the world's leading eye and ear specialists in Vienna, Berlin and Heidelberg. He had written two books, one on his Mediterranean voyage and another on the medical, literary and scientific insti-tutions of Austria which, despite its dry-sounding title, caused a considerable stir for its outspoken opinions. More important, however, he had been appointed medical adviser to the Irish Census of 1841 and when the medical statistics were published two years later they revealed data which was not being collected in any other country at the time. As a direct result he became Assistant Commissioner to the 1851 Census which has been described as one of the greatest demographic studies ever conducted and an indispensable source work for the Great

No 1 Merrion Square, Dublin, Oscar Wilde's childhood home, where his mother held her Saturday salon and his father had his surgery.

Famine. He held the same position for the two succeeding Censuses and he was knighted for his work on them in 1864 at the age of forty-nine.

At the start of his Dublin practice, finding that he was earning a considerable income, he felt he should make some provision for the free treatment of the city's poor who were suffering from diseases of the eye and ear which had become his speciality. In 1844 St Mark's Ophthalmic Hospital was

founded entirely at his expense. It showed a gen-
erosity and a sense of social justice in the father
which the son would later inherit and of which,
indeed, Oscar was proud, writing not long after his
father's death to a student friend: 'I have heard

Two eminent Irish
physicians share a
bottle of beer; William
Wilde (left) and
William Stokes (right).

Sir William Wilde in 1847 from a drawing by J. H. Maguire.

from many people of your father's liberality and noble spirit, so I know you will take interest in the report I send you of my father's hospital, which he built when he was only twenty-nine and not a rich man. It is a great memorial of his name.'

Alongside his medical work Sir William found time to indulge his interest in Celtic history and antiquities, took part in excavations and was responsible eventually for the three-volume *Catalogue of the Antiquities in the Museum of the Royal Irish Academy*, which is still in daily use. It was even said that he managed to combine business with pleasure and have himself paid by the impecunious peasants whom he treated with their telling of the ancient superstitions, legends, cures and charms of the country. Some of them doubtless found their way into his *Irish Popular Superstitions*, which he published in 1852 and dedicated to his newly-wed wife, but the remainder had to wait until she edited them for him more than a decade after his death, bringing unstinting praise from the young W. B. Yeats who himself would later draw on them extensively. Such was the extraordinary and energetic polymath who married Jane Francesca Elgee on 12 November 1851.

A mist of uncertainty has concealed Jane's birth until fairly recently, a mist, it should be said, which owed as much to her manipulation of history as history's laxity with its records. When she married she let it be known that she was 'around twenty-five' and 1826 was thereafter assumed to be the year of her birth. Since her father had died in August 1824 in India, this raised two possibilities: either she was illegitimate or she was not being strictly truthful about her age. It is highly probable that not even Oscar knew the truth, for when, under oath at his bankruptcy hearing in 1895 he was asked how old she was he replied, 'My mother's age is about sixty-five, I should think,' making her five years younger still. At any rate she would have had Lady Bracknell's wholehearted approval: 'You are perfectly right in making some slight alteration. Indeed, no woman should ever be quite accurate about her age. It looks so calculating.' The blunt fact, however, is that she was almost certainly born on 27 December 1821, the date she gave on her application for a grant from the Royal Literary Fund in 1888, by which time vanity and the romance of uncertainty had given way to the expediency of telling the truth. Nor was her need to embellish confined to her age: most probably christened Jane Frances Agnes, she soon dropped the third of her given names and converted the second into its Italian form to reinforce the family tradition that the Elgees were of Florentine origin and ultimately descended from or at least related to Dante Alighieri, of whose name Elgee was a corruption. The reality is less poetic: her great-grandfather had been a builder in County Durham, where the Elgees had long been labourers and bricklayers, and came to Ireland during an Irish building boom of the 1730s, prospered and settled in Dublin.

This family inclination for encouraging art to improve on nature passed in rude health to her son, Oscar, and subsequently to my father, Vyvyan, who maintained that on the Wilde side we were descended from a Dutch soldier of fortune, Colonel de Wilde who fought under William III; though what his Nationalist grandmother Jane would have said about the association with 'King Billy' does not bear thinking about. He also maintained that Oscar was named after the reigning King of Sweden on whom William Wilde had performed a successful operation for cataract and who, as a consequence, became Oscar's godfather. Pleasingly romantic explanations though these are, there is sadly no evidence for them at all, but since we are part of an age, in Oscar's words, 'with a disgusting appetite for facts', the record regrettably needs to be set straight.

Jane Elgee first caught the public eye in 1846 by sending poems under the pseudonym 'Speranza' to a weekly newspaper called *The Nation*. It had been founded four years before by the Young Irelanders, in particular Thomas Davis and Charles Gavan Duffy. The story of her Republican awakening relates that she was in the streets of Dublin one day in 1845 when a seemingly endless funeral cortège passed. Enquiring who had died and was being honoured by such a huge crowd, she was told that it was Thomas Davis, Nationalist and poet. 'That evening,' her own son said years later during his lecture tour of America, 'she bought and read his poems and knew for the first time the meaning of the word Country.' Even allowing for Oscar's habitual embellishment, it is probably close to the truth and her family, loyalist and with army connections, was thoroughly disapproving once they discovered that she was writing inflammatory anti-British verse for what it regarded as 'a seditious newspaper fit only for the fire'. By 1848, at the height of its popularity, it was said to have reached over 200,000 people a week, many of them through public readings, and Speranza had become firmly established as a regular contributor.

As the famine worsened and the Year of Revolution took hold of Europe, *The Nation* became increasingly outspoken. Duffy was finally arrested in July 1848 and two weeks later Jane wrote her most revolutionary piece yet, a leader entitled '*Jacta Alea Est*' ('The Die is Cast') which was little less than a call to arms against the English. The newspaper offices were promptly raided and closed down, and the issue seized. The leader was then used against Duffy at his trial, which was absurd since he had been in prison at the time. Tradition afterwards had it that Jane appeared in court and, at the moment the Attorney-General read it out, she stood up and said: 'I am the culprit if culprit there be,' but no newspaper reported such an incident at the time. Years later she wrote: 'I was amused at that imputed act of mine becoming historical . . . I shall leave it so – it will read well 100 years hence and if an illustrated history of Ireland is published no doubt I shall be immortalised in the act of addressing the court.' To surround oneself with an aura of unverifiable legend was a trait which Oscar inherited and improved on. On his arrival in America in 1882 he was asked by a New York reporter whether he had indeed walked down Piccadilly with a lily in his hand. 'To have done it was nothing,' he replied, 'but to make people think one had done it was a triumph.'

With the collapse of the Young Ireland movement and the temporary suppression of *The Nation* Jane reluctantly channelled her writing energies elsewhere. 'Writing for money is a very dull thing compared to writing for a revolution,' she admitted to a friend. A gifted linguist with a working knowledge of the major European languages, she set about translating Wilhelm Meinhold's gothic horror novel *Sidonia the Sorceress*, which Oscar would later read with relish and draw on for the darker elements of his own work. But if the responsibilities of family and marriage two years later dimmed the Republican ardour, it never quenched the fire entirely and her reputation lived on, especially in the hearts of those who had been forced to emigrate. When Oscar arrived in St Paul, Minnesota on St Patrick's Day 1882, the 'Professor of Aesthetics' found it to his advantage to play the Irish card for the first time since leaving Dublin and was introduced to his audience as 'the son of one of Ireland's noblest daughters'. By the time he arrived in San Francisco a

Oscar Wilde, aged about two, in a blue velvet dress. Coloured ambrotype.

Oscar's father, William Wilde, as a young man of twenty-eight in 1843 from a watercolour by Bernard Mulrenin.

Oscar's grandfather, Thomas Wilde, a country doctor in Castlereagh, County Roscommon in the early years of the 19th century. Colour miniature on ivory.

Right Jane Francesca Wilde as 'Speranza of *The Nation*' around 1848. A later engraving from the portrait by Stephen Catterson Smith.

Jane, Lady Wilde, as she had now become, aged forty-three in 1864 from a watercolour by Bernard Mulrenin.

A watercolour by Oscar in 1876 of the view from Moytura House, the Wildes' property on Lough Corrib. He inscribed it to Florrie Balcombe. His 'Alpine' landscape is a considerable improvement on Nature's rather flatter reality.

When his young sister, Isola, died aged ten in 1867 Oscar decorated an envelope and preserved in it a lock of her hair which he kept until his own death.

Mural 'Tight Lines' by Frank Miles inside Illaunroe, the family fishing lodge on Lough Fee. Frank and Oscar (L) are depicted as fishing cherubs.

Coloured lithograph of Wilde from a drawing by Thomas Maitland Cleland, 1882.

month later he had worked up a new lecture on 'The Irish Poets of '48' and was greeted enthusiastically as 'Speranza's Boy'. Jane still fired off the odd broadside about her downtrodden motherland over the next forty years but gradually left the job of putting the English in their place to her younger son, whose fifth-column tactics were ultimately to be more severely punished than her open warfare.

Jane's first child, William Charles Kingsbury, was born on 26 September 1852, prompting her to write to a friend 'As someone said seeing me over little saucepans in the nursery, "Alas the fates are cruel / Behold Speranza making gruel." ' The transition from firebrand to fireside was clearly not easy, but she was soon pregnant again and on 16 October 1854 her second child was born and was christened Oscar Fingal O'Flahertie Wills, a veritable mouthful of names by which he was embarrassed at school, proud of at university and dismissive of in later life, saying 'As one becomes famous, one sheds some of them, just as a balloonist, when rising higher sheds unnecessary ballast. All but two have already been thrown overboard. Soon I shall discard another and be known simply as "The Wilde" or "The Oscar".' If Willie had been christened with admirable restraint after his own father, Jane's father and Jane's mother's family name, reflecting the new domesticity, the latest arrival was an excuse to restate her Irishness. Oscar and Fingal were respectively son and father of Oisín, the third-century Celtic warrior-poet and O'fflahertie, as he would occasionally spell it, was in deference to her husband's links with 'the ferocious O'Flaherties of Galway'. Before his birth, Jane was reputed to have been sure that her baby was a girl and to have been disappointed when it was not, subsequently dressing Oscar in girl's clothes until he was ten which, it was said later, brought about his homosexuality. This facile explanation should be dismissed once and for all. In those days, and indeed well into the next century, children of both sexes were put in dresses or smocks until the age of about three, initially for practical reasons which anyone who has changed a nappy will appreciate. A photograph of Oscar at the age of about seven or eight shows him looking like any normal boy of his age. Apart from this there is nothing in Jane's letters of the time to intimate that she was anything but delighted with her new son and the daughter that she had longed for, Isola Emily Francesca, was delivered on 2 April 1857.

The gruel-making, if it had been any more than a figure of speech, certainly did not last long and less than a year after Oscar's birth the Wildes moved from 21 Westland Row behind Trinity College to an ample Georgian house round the corner at I Merrion Square and engaged six servants to run it. In addition they employed a French maid and a German governess, allowing the children to be tutored privately, especially in those two languages, in their early years. Oscar, Willie and Isola grew up

'Speranza' (Lady Wilde), a crayon drawing by J. Morosini c. 1870.

in what today would be comfortable, upper-middle-class professional surroundings, but with the significant difference that their parents were anything but conventional. Since the Act of Union the aristocracy had gravitated towards London, leaving the social scene in Dublin dominated by the liberal professions of law and medicine. Through the Wildes' house came a procession of doctors, lawyers, artists, literary men and academics from Trinity, as well as distinguished foreign visitors. One of these, who was in Dublin for the 1857 meeting of the British Association for the Advancement of Science, was Baron von Kraemer, Governor of Uppsala. From this encounter a thirty-year friendship developed between the families, and von Kraemer was so impressed by William Wilde both as medical man and antiquarian (he conducted an international expedition to the Aran Islands during the Association's meeting) that he recommended him for the Swedish Order of the North Star; it was bestowed on him during a visit to Sweden in 1862.

Jane's weekly 'conversazione', as she called it, was held from 4 p.m. to 7 p.m. on Saturdays and from about the mid-1860s she encouraged her children to mingle with the guests. In London ordinary parents would have considered such precocity unthinkable, but the style of Dublin was more akin to that of literary Paris than the socially hierarchical Metropolis and Jane was no ordinary mother. On one occasion when a friend asked her whether she

Opposite **Sir William Wilde** in his regalia as Chevalier of the Swedish Order of the North Star bestowed on him in 1862.

might bring a 'respectable' friend to one of Jane's afternoons, her hostess replied, 'You must never employ that description in this house; only tradespeople are respectable.' It must have been a regularly used epithet of denigration in the family as it crops up frequently with the same implied disapproval in Oscar's writings. Nor was he slow to follow her example. A few years later, while at Trinity College, he invited a fellow student back to Merrion Square with the words: 'Come home with me; I want to introduce you to my mother. We have founded a society for the suppression of virtue.' As children Oscar and Willie were also permitted to sit at the dinner table and to listen without contributing to the conversation, an early training in holding his tongue which, as Oscar explained, helped him to use it so effectively as an adult.

However, the Wilde family reputation, then as later, did not stop at the unconventional but tipped all too easily into the scandalous. William Wilde before his marriage had sowed more than his share of bachelor oats: while he had been away on his Mediterranean voyage in 1838 a young woman had given birth to his illegitimate son, Henry Wilson (Will's son); and two daughters were also born out of wedlock, Emily in 1847 and Mary in 1849. William, to his credit, provided for all of them. He paid for his son's education and medical studies, and finally took him into St Mark's Hospital as his assistant, where he distinguished himself as an oph-

Henry Wilson, Sir William Wilde's illegitimate son *c.* 1870.

thalmologist. The daughters, for the sake of appearances, were brought up by his brother, the Revd Ralph Wilde, as his wards but died together aged twenty-two and twenty-four in a tragic accident. At the end of a country ball near Monaghan one of the sisters' dresses caught alight as she danced past an open fire. The other, in an attempt to save her, was badly burned as well and both died of their injuries. Unfortunately their father's fondness for chasing petticoats did not stop with his marriage and in 1864 Sir William, as he had now become, was embroiled in a disastrous libel case involving a young female patient. Mary Travers, daughter of one of Sir William's medical colleagues, first came to him for earache in 1854. She was an attractive girl of nineteen with an unhappy home life. Sir William initially took a paternal interest in her and she was a frequent guest at the Wildes' house, but by 1860 the relationship had started to become more intimate. She fell out with Jane, became jealous of Sir William and began to behave in an erratic, unbalanced way. It culminated in her publishing a scurrilous pamphlet on Sir William and Lady Wilde thinly disguised as Dr and Mrs Quilp, in which Dr Quilp had chloroformed and raped one of his patients. For a time Merrion Square held out, but as Mary Travers's actions to draw attention to her situation became increasingly provocative and unhinged, Lady Wilde could take no more and wrote to the girl's father. When Mary discovered it she promptly sued Lady Wilde for libel and the whole story was the talk of Dublin for a week. The jury, although finding in her favour, set damages at one farthing but the costs of £2000 had to be borne by Sir William. The effect on his pocket was more severe than it was on his reputation, but from being at the pinnacle of his professional life he now seemed to go into decline and spent increasingly long periods at Moytura, the country house he had just built on the northern shore of Loch Corrib. We do not know the degree to which Oscar either knew what was happening or even was affected by it. Ironically, he was the same age as his own younger son would be when sexual scandals and a libel case were to bankrupt and destroy him thirty-one years later.

It was around this time that Willie and Oscar were sent off to board at Portora Royal School at Enniskillen. It enjoyed a superb academic reputation of which Oscar took advantage, excelling at Classics, and a good athletic one of which he did not, regarding the postures adopted by those who played cricket as 'indecent'. He had only been there two years when his young sister Isola died on 23 February 1867. He had been deeply attached to her and was profoundly affected by her death. She had been sent to stay with Sir William's sister in the country to recover from a bout of fever, but had a sudden relapse and died shortly after. The doctor who attended her described her as 'the most gifted and lovable child' he had ever known and

Sir William and Lady Wilde caricatured by *Punch* cartoonist Harry Furniss.

remembered Oscar as 'an affectionate, gentle, retiring, dreamy boy whose lonely and inconsolable grief found solace in long and frequent visits to his sister's grave in the village cemetery and in touching, boyish, poetic effusions.' The 'effusions' became more formalised later as 'Requiescat' the poem he wrote in her memory:

> Tread lightly, she is near
>   Under the snow,
> Speak gently, she can hear
>   The daisies grow.
>
> All her bright golden hair
>   Tarnished with rust,
> She that was young and fair
>   Fallen to dust.
>
> Lily-like, white as snow,
>   She hardly knew
> She was a woman, so
>   Sweetly she grew.
>
> Coffin-board, heavy stone,
>   Lie on her breast,
> I vex my heart alone,
>   She is at rest.
>
> Peace, Peace, she cannot hear
>   Lyre or sonnet,
> All my life's buried here,
>   Heap earth upon it.

More intimately, he preserved a lock of her hair in an envelope which he decorated himself in colour with their interlinked initials. It was among his few remaining possessions when he died.

In his last two years at Portora, 1870–1, he took the top prize in Classics each year and, more curiously, second prize for drawing in 1871. He showed a fondness for special editions of books and treasured in particular a large paper copy of Aeschylus' *Agamemnon* which he kept for years afterwards, until it was sold to pay his debts at the time of his trials. There was already a strong aesthetic sense at work, as well as an interest in his mother's Nationalist past (she had just published a poem 'To Ireland' in the *National Review*) as his first surviving letter from September 1868 shows:

> Darling Mama, The hamper came today, I never got such a jolly surprise, many thanks for it, it was more than kind of you to think of it. Please don't forget to send me the *National Review*. The flannel shirts you sent in the hamper are both Willie's, mine are one quite scarlet and the other lilac but it is too hot to wear them yet. You never told me anything about the publisher in Glasgow, what does he say? And have you written to Aunt Warren on the green note paper?

Aunt Warren was his mother's older sister and married to a captain in the British Army on whom

Scholars' board from Portora Royal School. Purser later became a distinguished Professor of Latin at Trinity College, but Wilde's name was effaced when he was imprisoned; it was not replaced until the 1930s.

the Nationalist significance of the green note-paper would not have been lost. She was fair game for the subversive amusement of mother and son.

On one occasion a group of students was discussing an ecclesiastical prosecution which had made a considerable stir at the time. One of his contemporaries, Sir Edward Sullivan, later editor of the *Book of Kells*, recalled: 'Oscar was present, and full of the mysterious nature of the Court of Arches: he told us there was nothing he would like better in after life than to be the hero of such a *cause célèbre* and go down to posterity as the defendant in such a case as *Regina* versus *Wilde*.' It was not the last time that he would make such a disturbingly premonitory remark in conversation.

He was neither exceptionally popular nor particularly disliked at school. His contemporaries admired his fluency with words and his prodigious memory which enabled him to read and absorb books at extraordinary speed. Even at school he earned himself a reputation as a talker and storyteller, exaggerating day-to-day incidents into tales of imagination and adventure for the amusement of his class-mates. His teachers equally were impressed with his passion for the Classics and his ability to make fluent oral translations from them at sight, and he crowned his other successes at Portora with the accolade of a Royal School Scholarship to Trinity College, Dublin in 1871 where he went a week before his seventeenth birthday. However, not even such academic brilliance was counterweight enough against his scandal when it came; Portora blacked out his name on the scholars' board and it was only regilded in the 1930s.

At Trinity Wilde came under the influence of two young dons, John Pentland Mahaffy and Robert Tyrrell. Mahaffy had the Chair of Ancient History and Tyrrell that of Latin. Oscar later confided to Frank Harris: 'I got my love of the Greek ideal and my intimate knowledge of the language at Trinity from Mahaffy and Tyrrell; they were Trinity to me. Mahaffy was especially valuable to me at that time. Though he was not as good a scholar as Tyrrell, he had been in Greece, had lived there and saturated himself with Greek thought and Greek feeling. Besides he took deliberately the artistic standpoint towards everything, which was coming more and more to be my standpoint. He was a delightful talker, too, a really great talker in a certain way – an artist in vivid words and eloquent pauses.' Although Harris has been frequently criticised for his biographical impressionism or, put more bluntly, his exaggerations and lies, in this case it is corroborated by a letter Wilde wrote to Mahaffy at the height of his theatrical successes: 'My dear Mahaffy, I am so pleased you liked the play, and thank you for your charming letter, all the more flattering to me as it comes not merely from a man of high and distinguished culture, but from one to whom I owe so much personally, from

The Revd John Pentland Mahaffy, Wilde's Classics tutor at Trinity, Dublin. Oscar kept up the friendship after going to Oxford and travelled twice with Mahaffy in Italy and Greece during his vacations.

my first and my best teacher, from the scholar who showed me how to love Greek things.'

Mahaffy was another polymath like his father, indeed one imagines there to have been a strong paternal–filial element in their relationship. He was an international marksman, had captained the Trinity cricket eleven, had a good knowledge of music, was an authority on old silver and furniture, and a connoisseur of claret and cigars. He was fluent in French, German and Italian, and most important of all was a remarkable conversationalist. Curiously, when Wilde was sent to prison in 1895 it was Tyrrell who signed a petition on his behalf and asked to be remembered to him, while Mahaffy simply distanced himself and said: 'We no longer speak of Mr Oscar Wilde.' In later years he modified his view and recalled Wilde as 'a delightful man to talk to on matters of scholarship, his views were always so fresh and unconventional'.

Oscar flourished at Trinity in an atmosphere at once intimidating and exhilarating to a young man fresh from school. Young adulthood beckoned and offered, in return for a modicum of responsibility, a sense of having crossed the divide between the teacher and the taught, to a place where ideas were discussed rather than spoon-fed. He did particularly well in his examinations, coming top of his year in Classics in the spring of 1872 and being elected in 1873 to what was the highest honour the College could bestow on an undergraduate – a

Foundation Scholarship. In his social life he continued to distinguish himself by a complete indifference to any form of competitive sport and a growing interest in art and literature outside his own field of the Classics. For his second year he shared rooms with his elder brother, Willie, in the 'Botany Bay' quadrangle. The rooms were grimy and ill-kept but in a prominent place in the sitting-room there would always be an unfinished landscape in oils on an easel which he would pretentiously call to the attention of any visitor. The aesthete was already beginning to recognise the value of the pose and even if the comment that it drew was not always complimentary, to be noticed was better than to be ignored. 'What odd chaps you painters are!' says Lord Henry to Basil Hallward in *The Picture of Dorian Gray*. 'You do anything in the world to gain a reputation. As soon as you have one, you seem to want to throw it away. It is silly of you, for there is only one thing in the world worse than being talked about, and that is not being talked about.'

But, as one of his contemporaries at Trinity later recounted, Oscar was not just a pallid young man with a pose. One day he read out a poem at which the class bully laughed sneeringly. Enraged, Wilde went up to him and demanded an explanation. The philistine then made the mistake of laughing again and Oscar slapped him across the face. Honour had to be satisfied with fists in the open air, but without a reputation for physical prowess, no one gave him the ghost of a chance. To universal astonishment he floored the bully with a series of powerful punches. Doubt has occasionally been cast on the authenticity of this anecdote, but a similar story told of him at Oxford, bodily throwing downstairs students who had come to break up his rooms, and the fact that Oscar was six feet three inches tall and powerfully built, give it the ring of truth.

One opponent from Trinity, Edward Carson, would take him on more than twenty years later in Court and destroy him, using the very weapon with which Oscar believed himself to be invincible – words. Carson was more conscientious and industrious than Wilde and disapproved of his flippant approach to life. He too worked for a Foundation Scholarship at the same time, but failed to be elected. Walking through the College one day with a friend, Wilde saw Carson and remarked, 'There goes a man destined to reach the very top of affairs.' 'Yes,' answered his companion, 'and one who will not hesitate to trample on his friends in getting there.'

In the first half of 1874 Wilde crowned his successes at Trinity with two final achievements. He won the College's Berkeley Gold Medal for Greek and was awarded a Demyship (scholarship) to Magdalen College, Oxford. The Medal, apart from the kudos that it brought to its winner, served a sadly practical function too: after his death his friends found a pawn ticket for it among his possessions. The move to Oxford was greeted by

The Berkeley Gold Medal for Greek won by Wilde in 1874 at Trinity. He would pawn and redeem it at moments of financial crisis throughout his life. The Greek inscription, a quotation from the *Iliad*, reads: 'Always to be the best.'

Tyrrell and Mahaffy with a mixture of pride that their teaching had borne such exceptional fruit and sadness at losing such an able pupil. On hearing the news, Mahaffy characteristically remarked: 'You're not quite clever enough for us here, Oscar. Better run up to Oxford.' Wilde, confident of his success before the results were announced, had not even bothered to take the Trinity third-year exams. After a brief trip to Geneva and Paris with his mother and brother he returned to Dublin, where he spent the last weeks of the summer helping Mahaffy correct the proofs of his forthcoming book *Social Life in Greece from Homer to Menander*.

There was an unconventional aspect to Mahaffy's interest in Greece which, if Oscar had not been aware of it before, would have become quite clear to him in performing this final service to his old tutor. Rare among contemporary scholars, he had dared to tackle the question of Greek homosexuality in his work. The book was published in November 1874 and acknowledged the help of 'Mr Oscar Wilde of Magdalen College', but because of adverse comment the passages on 'Greek love' were omitted from the second edition, as was the acknowledgement. Intellectual understanding, let alone public acceptance, of 'the love that dare not speak its name' was many decades away.

The day after his twentieth birthday Oscar Wilde entered Oxford with the confidence, if not the arrogance, of a scholar. 'The two great turning-

Above **Oscar (right) with cricketing friends taking refreshment.** *(Photo J. Guggenheim)*

Below **Oscar Wilde at Oxford in 1878.** *(Photo J. Guggenheim)*

points of my life were when my father sent me to Oxford, and when society sent me to prison,' he would write from Reading Gaol. Although it was almost certainly Mahaffy who had encouraged him to sit the exam, there was probably encouragement from his father as well, not least because he had noticed with growing apprehension his son's leaning towards the Catholic Church in his home city. If so, it was a singularly ill-informed decision, since it delivered him directly into the enemy's hands. Oxford since the 1830s had been the centre of a movement to stem the tide of Protestantism in the Anglican Church and bring it closer to its Catholic roots. The Oxford Movement in the 1850s had seen a spate of conversions to Rome, in particular those of Newman and Manning (both later to become cardinals) and its influence by the time Wilde arrived was as strong as ever. Oscar toyed with the idea of 'going over' throughout his time at Oxford, encouraged by a close college friend, David Hunter Blair, who himself converted in spectacular fashion while in Rome to see Manning first don his cardinal's hat. What it was, precisely, which attracted him to Catholicism is difficult to say: one thing is certain – it was not religious fervour. In a revealing letter written in the spring of 1877 to another friend, William Ward, Oscar is frank about his reasons:

Wilde won the Newdigate Prize for poetry with 'Ravenna' in 1878. The bust in the foreground is of Augustus Caesar, left by a Magdalen don, Dr Daubeny, to the next undergraduate at the college to win the prize. His brother Willie is seated at the front; between them is possibly their mother, Lady Wilde.

If I could hope that the Church would wake in me some earnestness and purity I would go over *as a luxury*, if for no better reasons. But I can hardly hope it would, and to go over to Rome would be to sacrifice and give up my two great gods 'Money and Ambition'. Still I get so wretched and low and troubled that in some desperate mood I will seek the shelter of a Church which simply enthralls me by its fascination.

For the time being the fascination had to be satisfied by becoming a freemason with its quasi-religious rituals and fancy dress and he was admitted to the Apollo University Lodge in February 1875.

The degree for which Wilde had chosen to read was naturally enough Classics, or *Literae Humaniores* as it is still called, and while the concentration was on Greek and Latin language and literature, it was designed, as the name suggests, to produce Humanists rather than mere Classicists. He would have been expected to study modern philosophy, philology and history, as well as ancient texts. The notebooks which he kept during his four-year course, and which miraculously have survived, bear this out and show, too, how widely read he was in both English and European literature. It is all too easy to forget, given that the popular view of Wilde is now dominated by his later life-style and the scandal which overtook and destroyed him, what an exceptional scholar he was. In both parts of his degree, Honour Moderations in 1876 and Greats in 1878 he was awarded a First, and at the viva voce his examiners were said to have spent more time congratulating him on his performance than questioning him about his written papers.

Social life at Oxford was radically different from what he had enjoyed in Dublin. Now that he had his own rooms without having to share with his brother, he took particular care in furnishing them. There were several portraits of Manning and the Pope adorning the walls, as well as a considerable quantity of blue and white china, the latter occasioning one of the earliest and most repeated of early Wildeisms, 'I find it harder and

Oscar Wilde with his two closest Oxford friends, Reginald 'Kitten' Harding (*left*) and William 'Bouncer' Ward (*centre*), Wilde's closest friends at Oxford, March 1876. His letters to them have survived and give an invaluable account of his life at University.
(*Photo Hills & Saunders*)

Above **Wilde with an unidentified Oxford friend, 1875.**
(*Photo Hills & Saunders*)

Below **Wilde with an undergraduate friend, Arnold Fitzgerald, 1875.**
(*Photo Hills & Saunders*)

Above Oscar with the Magdalen College cricket club, the strictly non-playing member.

Opposite Oscar with a group of Magdalen friends, March 1876: back left to right A. F. Peyton, C. H. Tindal, Wilde; front left to right C. H. Lindon, T. T. Peyton. *(Photo Hills & Saunders)*

Below The cloisters of Magdalen College, a photograph taken during Wilde's time there.

Oscar Wilde (in centre row
with dark suit and bowler hat) with a
group of college friends in the
cloisters of Magdalen, summer 1876.
William Ward, also wearing a bowler,
is second on his left.

Aesthetic Bridegroom: It is quite consummate is it not?

Intense Bride: It is indeed! Oh, Algernon, let us live up to it!

George du Maurier started caricaturing the Aesthetic movement in *Punch* in 1879. This sketch entitled 'The Six-Mark Tea-Pot' was undoubtedly inspired by Oscar's remark about blue china.

harder every day to live up to my blue china.' Whether or not it was first uttered for general release is not known, but it rapidly did the rounds and was even condemned one Sunday by the preacher at the University Church as 'a form of heathenism which it is our bounden duty to fight against and to crush out if possible'. Oscar professed himself delighted at the typical English way in which his ideas were misunderstood and marked down the experience for future use. But outraging the establishment was a dangerous game when overplayed and, fifteen years on, the heathenism of *Dorian Gray* would nearly capsize him.

If Oxford gave Wilde the freedom from the family constraints of Dublin, it also encouraged him to build entirely new friendships. Apart from David Hunter Blair, his intimates were Reginald 'Kitten' Harding and William 'Bouncer' Ward in whose company, like any modern undergraduate, he wasted time constructively. Hunter Blair left a sympathetic and telling memoir of their time together:

When the punch had been drunk and the pipes smoked out, the lights extinguished the piano closed and the merry guests dispersed, at no very unreasonably late hour, there followed an hour or two which still, after sixty long years, linger vividly in my memory. Round the fire gathered Wilde, William Ward – known to us all as 'Bouncer'

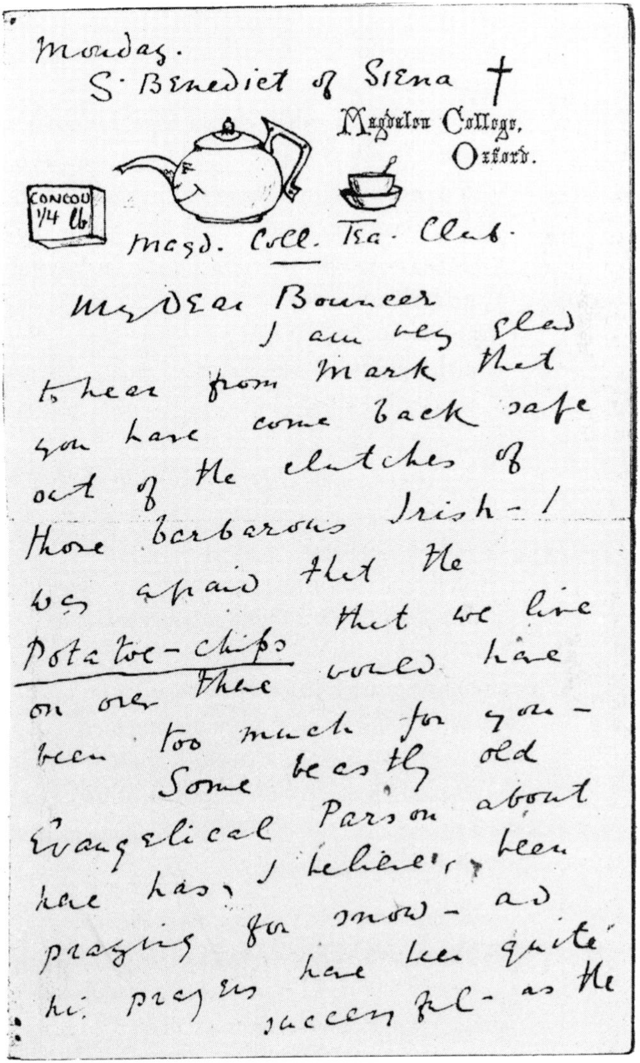

Monday.

S. Benedict of Siena ✝

Magdalen College,
Oxford.

Magd. Coll. Tea Club.

My Dear Bouncer
                    I am very glad
to hear from Mark that
you have come back safe
out of the clutches of
those barbarous Irish—!
I was afraid that the
Potatoe-chips that we live
on over there would have
been too much for you—
        Some beastly old
Evangelical Parson about
here has, I believe, been
praying for snow—and
his prayers have been quite
        successful—as the

Letter to William Ward, March 1876; the Magdalen College Tea Club existed only in Oscar's imagination.

41

— and I; just we three, and talked and talked as boys will, about everything and other things as well. Oscar was always the protagonist in these midnight conversations, pouring out a flood of paradoxes, untenable propositions, quaint comments on men and things; and sometimes, like Silas Wegg 'dropping into poetry', spouting yards of verse, either his own or that of other poets he favoured, and spouting it uncommonly well. We listened and applauded and protested against some of his preposterous theories.

'You talk a lot about yourself, Oscar,' said Ward, 'and of all the things you would like to achieve. But you never say what you are going to do with your life. You who have twice as much brains in that ridiculous head of yours as both of us put together — what are you going to do with them?'

'God knows,' said Oscar, serious for a moment. 'I won't be a dried up Oxford don, anyhow. I'll be a poet, a writer, a dramatist. Somehow or other I'll be famous, and if not famous, notorious.'

It was an unfortunate premonition. He achieved it all and in exactly that order.

What Dublin had sowed flowered intellectually in Oxford. He made the acquaintance of both

John Ruskin, Slade Professor of Fine Art and Walter Pater, Fellow of Brasenose College, on whose theories of art and aesthetics he was to base his own flamboyant style. Each appealed to a different Wilde: Ruskin to the intellectual, the noble, the high minded; Pater, more insidiously, to the sensual, the decadent, the mystical. Oscar, having attended Ruskin's lectures on Florentine Aesthetics in his first term, was soon persuaded to take part in his new mentor's practical beautification of the countryside and found himself rising at dawn to help build a country road. The reward was less in the toil than in the pleasure of breakfasting with Ruskin afterwards. The enthusiasm, however, soon waned, the road sank back into Hinksey Marsh but the friendship flourished. When Wilde sent him a copy of *The Happy Prince* in 1888 he accompanied it with a note: 'The dearest memories of my Oxford days are my walks and talks with you and from you I learned nothing but what was good. . . . There is in you something of prophet, of priest, and of poet.'

Pater was less uplifting for the soul but dangerously attractive to the senses. Wilde had read his *Studies in the History of the Renaissance* soon after his arrival in Oxford and found himself disturbingly attuned to its philosophies especially those in the 'Conclusion' in which Pater had written that 'Not the fruit of experience but experience itself is the end' and continued: 'To burn always with this hard

M. Oscar Fingal O'Flahertie Wills Wilde 1877

Your Favorite

1. Color? Couleur de rose (after a rose).
2. Flower? Lilium Auratum
3. Tree? Stone Pine and Lemon Tree
4. Object in Nature? The sea. (when there are no bathing machines)
5. Hour in the Day? Post Hour.
6. Season of the Year? Beginning of autumn.
7. Perfume? almond-blossoms
8. Gem? Sapphire in winter, diamond in summer.
9. Style of Beauty? that of Guido St. Sebastian and of the "Venus of Melos"
10. Names, Male and Female? Eucharis in cell, Florence cecil.
11. Painters? Fra Angelico: Turner: Coreggio.
12. Musicians? Mozart. Gounod. Chopin
13. Piece of Sculpture? Apoxyomenos of Vatican.
14. Poets? Euripedes Keats. Theocritus and myself.
15. Poetesses? Sappho and Lady Wilde
16. Prose Authors? Plato and John Ruskin.
17. Character in Romance? Achilles: Nausicaa
18. .... in History? Dr. Newman. Alexander.
19. Book to take up for an hour? I never take up books for an hour.
20. What Book (not religious) would you part with last? my Euripides.

Pages from an American 'Confession Album' filled out by Wilde in 1877. There is a disturbingly premoniti

21. What epoch would you choose to have lived in? _He Italian Renaissance._

22. Where would you like to live? _Florence and Rome._

23. What is your favorite amusement? _writing sonnets, and Riding._

24. What is your favorite occupation? _reading my own sonnets._

25. What trait of character do you most admire in man? _the power of attracting friends_

26. What trait of character do you most admire in woman? _the power of becoming either a Cleopatra, or a St. Catherine_

27. What trait of character do you most detest in each? _Vanity: self-esteem: conceitedness_

28. If not yourself, who would you rather be? _a Cardinal of the Catholic Church —_

29. What is your idea of happiness? _absolute power over men's minds, even if accompanied by chronic toothache._

30. What is your idea of misery? _living a poor and respectable life in an obscure village._

31. What is your bête noir? _a thorough Irish Protestant._

32. "   "   dream? _getting my hair cut_

33. What is your favorite game? _Snipe and Lawn Tennis._

34. What do you believe to be your distinguishing characteristics? ~~xxxxxx~~ _moderate self-esteem_

35. If married, what do you believe to be the distinguishing characteristics of your better-half? _Devotion to her husband_

36. What is the sublimest passions of which human nature is capable? _asceticism: ambition_

37. What are the sweetest words in the world? _Well Done!_

38. What are the saddest words? _Failure._

39. What is your aim in life? _Success: fame or even notoriety_

40. What is your motto?

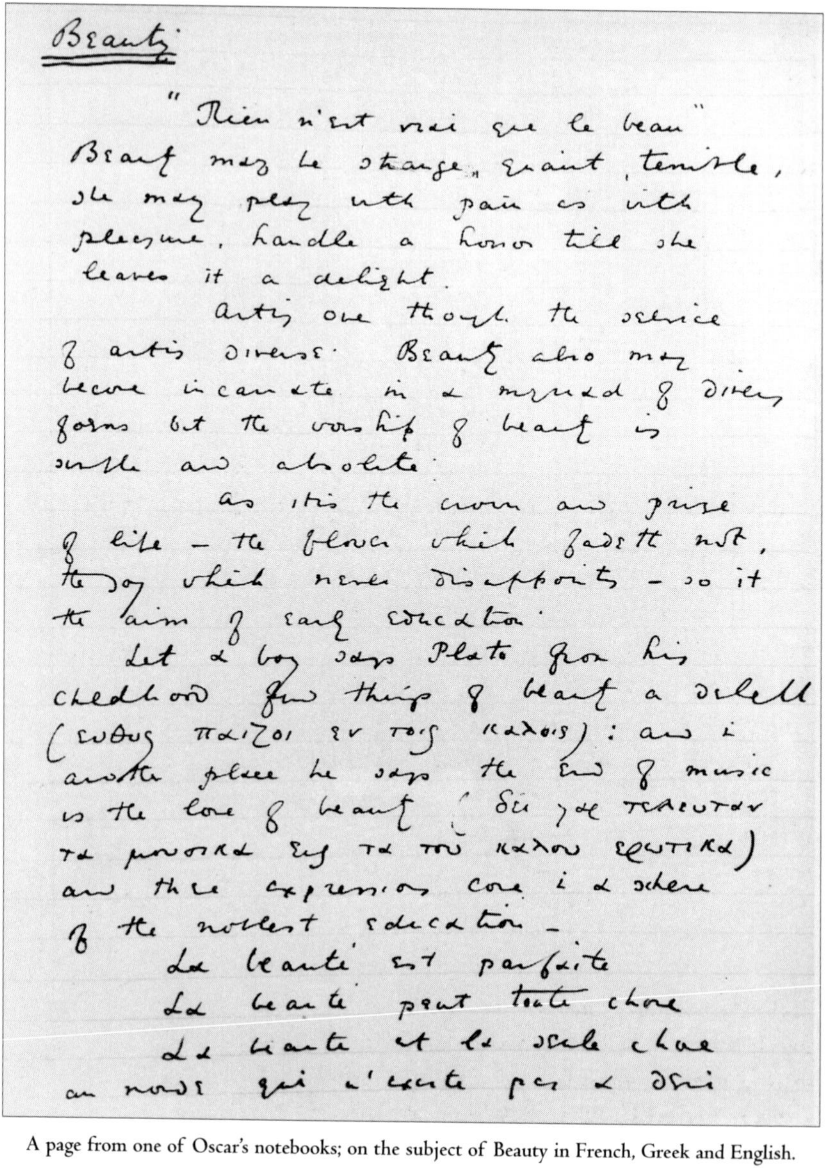

Beauty

"Rien n'est vrai que le beau"
Beauty may be strange, quaint, terrible,
she may play with pain as with
pleasure, handle a horror till she
leaves it a delight.

Artists are though the service
of artists diverse: Beauty also may
become incarnate in a myriad of divers
forms but the worship of beauty is
simple and absolute.

As it is the crown and prize
of life — the flower which fadeth not,
the joy which never disappoints — so it
the aim of early education.

Let a boy says Plato from his
childhood find things of beauty a delight
(εὐθὺς παίζοι ἐν τοῖς καλοῖς): and in
another place he says the end of music
is the love of beauty (δεῖ γὰρ τελευτᾶν
τὰ μουσικὰ εἰς τὰ τοῦ καλοῦ ἐρωτικά)
and these expressions come in a scheme
of the noblest education —

La beauté est parfaite
La beauté peut toute chose
La beauté est la seule chose
au monde qui n'existe pas à demi

gem-like flame, to maintain this ecstacy, is success in life.' He also declared that enrichment of our given lifespan consisted of 'getting as many pulsations as possible into the given time' and of having 'the desire for beauty, the love of art for its own sake'. Writing from prison, Wilde would refer to it as 'that book which has had such a strange influence over my life'. There were echoes of Dorian Gray's total surrender to the poisoned perfection of the novel Lord Henry gives him in which 'The life of the senses was described in the terms of mystical philosophy'.

But the excitement of new teachings did not lead Oscar to abandon old friends and he still found time for Mahaffy, with whom he travelled to Italy in the summer of 1875. They visited Florence, Venice, Padua, Verona and Milan, where he decreed the cathedral 'an awful failure' but admired Bernardino Luini's Madonna at the Brera Gallery and a seventh-century Irish manuscript at the Ambrosian Library. 'Venice,' he wrote to his mother, 'in beauty of architecture and colour is beyond description.' Ruskin's teaching had fired him with the desire to experience the Renaissance for himself and his old tutor had provided the opportunity.

Back in Dublin his father's health was slowly failing. It was as if he had burned himself out prematurely with overwork and his multifarious interests, and on 19 April 1876 he died. The state of his finances was far worse than anyone could have suspected; Sir William had been living off his capital and both the family home on Merrion Square and Moytura House on Loch Corrib were heavily mortgaged, so the future for Oscar's mother looked grim. However, Henry Wilson, the illegitimate son, paid off the debt on Merrion Square, enabling Jane and Willie to continue living there, and Oscar's contingent worries about money gave way to sadness that his father had not witnessed the result of his Moderation exams two months later: 'My father would have been so pleased about it. It has robbed me of any real pleasure in my First.'

Opposite **Oscar Wilde in Greek national costume during his trip to Greece with Mahaffy in April 1877.** *(Photo P. Moraites, Athens)*

Below **Wilde with unidentified companion around 1877.** *(Photo W. Savage, Winchester)*

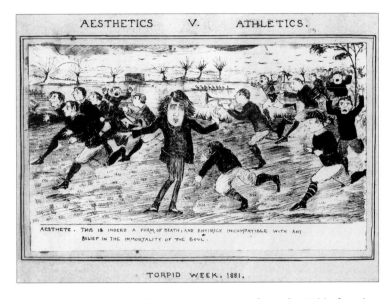

AESTHETICS   V.   ATHLETICS.

AESTHETE. THIS IS INDEED A FORM OF DEATH, AND ENTIRELY INCOMPATIBLE WITH ANY
BELIEF IN THE IMMORTALITY OF THE SOUL.

TORPID WEEK, 1881.

Above **Aesthetics vs. Athletics.** An 1881 view of the 'Professor of Aesthetics' who complains of the hearty Oxford oarsmen: 'This is indeed a form of death, and entirely incompatible with any belief in the immortality of the soul.'

Opposite **Wilde in the costume of Prince Rupert 'with plum-coloured breeches and silk stockings'** in which he attended an Oxford fancy dress ball 1 May 1878. *(Photo J. Guggenheim)*

That summer was significant for Wilde for other reasons as well: a close friendship developed with a young portrait painter living in London, Frank Miles; and he appears to have fallen in love with Florence Balcombe. Miles was already well introduced into London society through his sketching or painting of the great and the beautiful, and it was in his studio that Wilde first met Lillie Langtry. Given his self-confessed ambition at the time, the friendship cannot have been entirely unconnected with Wilde's future social aspirations. Nevertheless, there was undoubtedly a strong affection between them as they spent several weeks together at the Mileses' family house in

Nottingham and at the Wildes' country retreat in Connemara, fishing and shooting.

The relationship with Florrie, if we believe the parting letters he wrote to her two years later on her engagement to Bram Stoker, was truly romantic: 'She is just seventeen with the most perfectly beautiful face I ever saw and not a sixpence of money,' he wrote to William Ward. Later that summer he painted a water-colour landscape of the view from Moytura House which he gave her; and at Christmas he presented her with a small gold cross with his name inscribed on it. When she made her stage début in 1881 he sent her anonymously through Ellen Terry, who was in the lead, a crown of flowers to wear: 'I should like to think she was wearing something of mine the first night she comes on the stage, that anything of mine should touch her. She thinks I never loved her, thinks I forget. My God how could I!'

While waiting for Miles to arrive in August, Wilde helped Mahaffy to correct the proofs of his next book, *Rambles and Studies in Greece*, and the renewed contact was to have some unexpected consequences. The following spring, still attracted by Catholicism and agonising over his possible conversion, Wilde agreed to join Hunter Blair and Ward in Rome. Mahaffy, on a voyage to Greece, took Wilde with him as far as Genoa and had by then persuaded him that Paganism was preferable to Popery, so Wilde continued with Mahaffy's party through Ravenna to Greece. Not wishing to upset his friends, however, he

Florence Balcombe, Oscar's first love and sketched by him about 1877.

passed by Rome on his return, where Hunter Blair had arranged a private audience with Pius IX. Wilde was deeply moved but remained unconverted, arrived back at Magdalen a month late, was sent down for the rest of the term and fined. 'I was sent down from Oxford for being the first undergraduate to visit Olympia,' he later complained. He went at once to London, where he attended and wrote a review of the opening of the Grosvenor Gallery, his first published piece of prose, before retreating to Dublin. A copy of the review he sent calculatingly to Walter Pater, who replied with effusive praise and invited Wilde to call as soon as he was back in Oxford. As a further blow to any idea of becoming a Catholic, his half-brother Henry Wilson died suddenly and the little that he bequeathed Oscar (£100 and his half share in the Connemara fishing lodge) was conditional on his remaining a Protestant for five years; brother Willie, with no Popish leanings, received £2000.

His last year at Magdalen he spent 'reading hard for a Fourth' but still found time to enter for the University poetry prize – the Newdigate. By extraordinary coincidence the subject for 1878 was 'Ravenna' and he handed in his piece a year to the day after he had entered its walls with Mahaffy. On 10 June the Newdigate prize was declared his and on 19 July his First in Greats was announced by the examiners, who considered his papers the most outstanding of his year. So ended, in a blaze of glory, the making of the 'Professor of Aesthetics', as he would style himself.

Oscar sketched by Frank Miles while they were sharing rooms in London's Tite Street in 1881.

MR. WILLIAM WILDE.

Oscar's brother, Willie Wilde, a drama critic caricatured by Alfred Bryan in *The Entr'acte*, 26 March 1881.

Opposite **Down from Oxford, Oscar changed hearty tweed for aesthetic velvet.** *(Photo Elliot & Fry, London)*

MR. OSCAR WILDE.

QUITE TOO UTTERLY ECSTATIC.

Oscar, still only the author of a few poems and a review or two, caricatured by Alfred Bryan in *The Entr'acte*, 26 March 1881.

Oscar Wilde now had his eyes on London and went to live with his friend Frank Miles in Salisbury Street off the Strand. His mother's salon in Dublin, his academic success, his entrée into society through Miles had prepared the ground perfectly, but one important ingredient was lacking – money. He had a capital sum of about £2500, realised from the sale of some inherited properties, but the income from it certainly would not allow him to entertain in such a style as to gain him a foothold on the social ladder.

'To get into the best society, nowadays, one has either to feed people, amuse people, or shock people – that is all. A man who can dominate a London dinner-table can dominate the world,' explains Lord Illingworth so aptly in *A Woman of No Importance*. If he could not afford to feed them, at least he could amuse and shock them, so he was thrown back on his wits, or more precisely his Irish wit, and he set about talking himself into London society. He made the acquaintance of the leading actresses and Professional Beauties of the time, Ellen Terry, Lillie Langtry and the great Sarah Bernhardt, attended their first nights and their soirées, and published sonnets to them.

Paying court to them on paper, though, was not enough. The sort of reputation that he wanted to establish had to be fuelled by legend and hearsay. So when 'La divine Sarah' came to London with the Comédie-Française he met her at Folkestone with

The 'Professor of Aesthetics' in 1881, before his departure on the American lecture tour. *(Photos Elliot & Fry, London)*

'The Bard of Beauty' by Alfred Thompson from *Time*, April 1880, one of the earliest caricatures of Oscar offering a sonnet to Ellen Terry and a triolet to Sarah Bernhardt.

Above **Sarah Bernhardt came to London with the Comédie-Française in June 1879 and Oscar courted her with armfuls of lilies at Folkestone and a sonnet for her performance in *Phèdre*.**

Left top **Ellen Terry, the finest English actress of her time and another recipient of Wilde's early poetry.** *(Photo Alex Bassano, London)*

Left middle **Caricature of Wilde by Linley Sambourne from *Punch*, 25 June 1881, shortly after publication of his *Poems* and the first in association with a sunflower.**

Left bottom **Lillie Langtry, one of the Professional Beauties of the 1880s, whom Oscar used to further his early career, but to whom he grew more attached than he admitted.**

an armful of Madonna lilies, with which he carpeted the ground at her feet, and made the waiting crowd cheer her to the train. His attentions to 'the Jersey Lily' were even more public and varied, from accompanying her to classical lectures for the improvement of her education to sleeping on her doorstep to catch a glimpse of her returning early one morning. Helen Modjeska, the Polish actress, was sceptical: 'What has he done, this young man, that one meets him everywhere? Oh yes, he talks well, but what has he *done*? He has written nothing, he does not sing or paint or act – he does nothing but talk. I do not understand.' But she too was won over by the 'voice the texture of brown velvet played like a cello' as a contemporary put it and even the Prince of Wales asked to meet him. 'Not to know Mr Wilde', he said, 'is not to be known.'

Wilde himself was conscious of the lack of discernable success. He wrote to Reggie Harding at the end of 1879 saying that he had been to Hampshire 'to kill time and pheasants and the *ennui* of not having set the world quite on fire as yet', but added characteristically: 'I am going tonight with Ruskin to see Irving as Shylock and afterwards to the Millais Ball,' as he continued to network his way about London.

He did, however, start committing more to paper than the odd sonnet, and by the autumn of 1880 he had finished and privately printed his first play, *Vera; or The Nihilists*. Its subject was surprisingly subversive from one who desired more to ingratiate himself with an established order than to destroy it, but Republicanism was modish and the Home Rule movement in Ireland was gathering momentum, so Oscar rode along in the hope of being able to improve his finances. This was particularly necessary since he and Frank Miles had now moved to a house in the newly fashionable Tite Street in Chelsea, a luxury supported to a large extent by Miles's family. By March 1881 the play had taken on an unexpected topicality through the murder of Czar Alexander II and its première was scheduled for December, but a second assassination, that of President Garfield in September, led to a change of public mood and Wilde felt it prudent to postpone the opening. It was a diplomatic move, considering the Prince of Wales was married to the new Czarina's sister. In the end *Vera* was produced in New York in August 1883, where it played to small houses for only a week, after being slated by the critics; the *New York Herald* described it as 'long-drawn dramatic rot'.

Frank Miles, with whom Wilde shared rooms in London from 1879 to 1881. Miles was an artist from whose connections in London society Oscar benefited considerably.

Slightly more successful, though not without its critics and even its dramatic moment, was the publication 1881 of a volume simply entitled *Poems*. Published by David Bogue but paid for by the author, it came out in July 1881 to a mixed critical reception. *Punch* referred to it as 'Swinburne and water'; the *Saturday Review* said it was 'marred everywhere by imitation, insincerity and bad taste'. Undeterred, Oscar sent copies to anyone of note whom he knew, including Algernon Swinburne, Robert Browning, Matthew Arnold and the Prime Minister, William Gladstone. To his delight a copy was even solicited by the Oxford Union, but with unfortunate consequences. On its reception an undergraduate, Oliver Elton, denounced the work publicly as thin, immoral but above all derivative, pointing to Wilde's 'borrowings', and moved a motion that it should be rejected. It was; and as a result the Union, to its embarrassment, was forced to return the volume to its author. A dislike of Wilde's flamboyant style and growing reputation as an aesthetic poseur was undoubtedly at the root of this farce. Why else would a second-year student have taken notice of what was otherwise a fairly routine acquisition? Envy clothes itself in curious forms. Elton, a Classical scholar like Wilde before him, had only managed a Second in his Moderations that summer and, mindful that this Irish peacock had distinguished himself with a double First, would have been doubly galled. It was not the last time that Oscar would feel the lash of public disapproval from 'the smaller natures and the meaner minds' as he later put it. Criticism also came from an unexpected quarter: the sinful indulgence that Frank Miles's clergyman father read into *Poems* caused him deep concern. He wrote pleading with his son to have nothing further to do with

Wilde. Angry and against his will, Oscar was forced to move out of their shared house.

Meanwhile he had been 'appearing' regularly since early 1880 in the columns of *Punch* as Jellaby Postlethwaite, the 'quite too utterly' aesthetic poet. The caricatures by George du Maurier were essentially good-natured fun at the expense of the Aesthetes and included Maudle the painter and Prigsby the art critic under the general heading of Nincompoopiana. Oscar looked on in amused toleration; all public exposure fuelled his campaign of self-promotion and, though he could not know it, this was to lead indirectly to a highly profitable year in America.

In April 1881 a new Gilbert and Sullivan opera, *Patience*, opened in London. It played along with the public delight in seeing the rarified world of the Aesthetic movement lampooned. Reginald Bunthorne and Archibald Grosvenor, its two main aesthetic protagonists, were composite characters, the one 'fleshly' and the other 'spiritual'. Neither represented Wilde directly, yet both had elements of him and if the theatre audiences wanted to believe that Bunthorne *was* Wilde, what matter? In September, the producer Richard D'Oyly Carte opened *Patience* in New York with a success as great as in London. A North-American tour was planned for the following year and in October Carte (supposedly at the suggestion of Sarah Bernhardt) proposed a series of lectures to Wilde which would give

The master photographer himself.

New York photographers paid large sums to photograph celebrities and sell the prints. Wilde's manager waived the fee for Napoleon Sarony who shot Wilde in at least 27 poses, the numbers generally appearing in odd places on the prints themselves.

(Bold numbers in the margins indicate the original sequence, with the exception of no 4 which is conjecture.)

Admiration was by no means universal; his mother wrote in February 1882: 'The photographs are greatly admired here – especially the standing figure in the fur coat – they are beautifully executed. I only object to the hair parted in the centre.'

He was very attached to his fur coat which his brother sold when he was in prison: 'It was all over America with me, it was at all my first nights, it knows me perfectly, and I really want it.'

'I have two secretaries, one to write my autograph and answer the hundreds of letters that come begging for it. Another whose hair is brown to send locks of his own hair to the young ladies who write asking for mine; he is rapidly becoming bald.'

'The imagination will concentrate itself on the waistcoat.
Waistcoats will show whether a man can admire poetry or not.'

'Men should dress more in velvet as it catches the light and shade, while broadcloth is ugly as it does not absorb the light. Trousers become dirty in the street; knee-breeches are more comfortable and convenient – prettier to look at too . . . low shoes and silk stockings should be used in the drawing-room.'

'Great success here: nothing like it since Dickens, they tell me. I am torn in bits by Society. . .
Crowds wait for my carriage. I wave a gloved hand and an ivory cane and they cheer.'

'The large hat of the last century was sensible and useful, and nothing is more graceful in the world than a broad-brimmed hat. . . We have lost the art of draping the human form and the cloak is the simplest and most beautiful drapery ever devised.'

26.

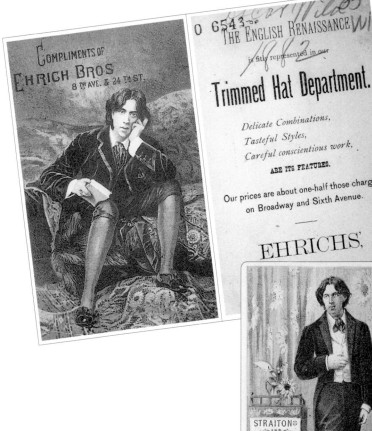

Compliments of
EHRICH BROS
8 TH AVE. & 24 TH ST.

O 6543 THE ENGLISH RENAISSANCE
is fitly represented in our

Trimmed Hat Department.

Delicate Combinations,
Tasteful Styles,
Careful conscientious work,
ARE ITS FEATURES.

Our prices are about one-half those charged
on Broadway and Sixth Avenue.

EHRICHS,

STRAITON
AND
STORM'S
NEW CIGARS.

AESTHETIC
SUN-FLOWER
TOO TOO
CAPADURA PATIENCE

DEALERS SUPPLIED BY
R.C. BROWN & CO.
NEW YORK.

OSCAR WILDE.

Some examples of trade cards in which
Oscar became the unwitting endorser of
such diverse products as trimmed hats and
cigars. Sarony sued the Burrow Giles
Lithographic Co. who printed Ehrlich's card
using his images – numbers 11 and 18. He
won and the case established the legal basis
for American photographic copyright.

These two portraits of Wilde were also taken by Sarony but not at the same time as the main 'aesthetic' series. They were probably taken in August 1883 when he returned to New York for the disastrous staging of his first play *Vera*.

him a platform to start his career seriously and give the Americans a taste of what the Aesthetes were. Dickens had done such a tour fifteen years before to huge acclaim, but only towards the end of his life. The chance for Wilde to make an early reputation internationally, as well as some badly needed money, was worth the risk of ridicule. He had been forced by his rupture with Miles to move in with his mother, who herself was in straitened circumstances and had been obliged to give up the family home in Dublin and come to London.

Opposite and above **Photographic portraits of Wilde, probably taken in summer 1882.** *(Photos Van der Weyde, New York)*

By December the finances had been agreed and Wilde had prepared himself for the part by having his tailor make him some suitably aesthetic lecturing outfits and a heavy fur-lined coat. The essentials, as he saw them, being ready, he set sail on 24 December for New York without a word of a lecture written. America had been primed and on his arrival he was besieged by reporters wanting appropriately intense quotations from what they expected to be a limp-wristed, lily-toting fop. Their surprise was universal. The *New York Tribune* wrote:

Caricature of Wilde with lily during the American tour by unknown artist.

> The most striking thing about the poet's appearance is his height, which is several inches over six feet, and the next thing to attract attention is his hair which is of dark brown colour, and falls down upon his

Top right The announcement of Oscar's first lecture on his arrival in New York.

Above An idealised Oscar looking about ten years younger than his age addresses the matrons of New York. *Frank Leslie's Illustrated Newspaper*, 21 January 1882.

Left Oscar, armed with his *Poems* in one hand, hopes to storm America, though what Zola's *Nana* is doing in the other remains unclear. *Society*, 18 January 1882.

Top left For some, Oscar's arrival in America was not so welcome. *The Judge*, January 1882

Brother Jonathan, epitome of the American backwoods, is none too sure about England's latest export. Caricature by Arthur Bryan in *The Entr'acte*, 21 January 1882.

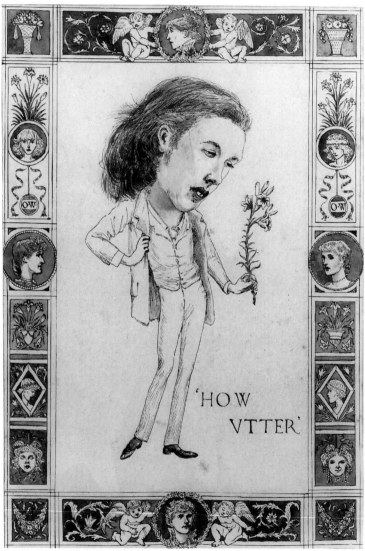

'HOW VTTER'

Oscar surrounded by Professional Beauties contemplates his favourite flower. Published by Thomas Shrimpton, Oxford, c. 1881 and drawn by J. B. B. Nichols, who himself won the Newdigate Poetry Prize in 1883.

Left Very rare ten-cent pamphlet, lampooning the aesthetic Wilde, published in New York 1882.

Right Wilde declared the miners of Leadville, Colorado, to be the best-dressed men in America. Thomas Nast in *Harpers Bazar*, 10 June 1882.

above Left In his lecture on 'The Decorative Arts' Wilde pronounced: 'There is one article of furniture . . that for absolutely horrid ugliness surpasses anything I have seen – the cast iron American stove.' Thomas Nast replied for the stove in *Harpers Weekly*, 2 September 1882.

above right During his American tour Wilde was even used to sell musical scores.

Above **Drawing by James Edward Kelly of Wilde with the artist's son, January 1882.**

Opposite **When Wilde trimmed his aesthetic locks in March 1882, the press foresaw an amusing sequel to short hair and breeches; ironically thirteen years later conjecture became reality.** *Illustrated Sporting and Dramatic News, 1883.*

shoulders. . . . When he laughs his lips part widely and show a shining row of upper teeth which are superlatively white. . . . His eyes are blue, or light gray, and instead of being 'dreamy' as some of his admirers have imagined them to be, they are bright and quick. . . . Instead of having a small delicate hand only fit to caress a lily, his fingers are long and when doubled up would hit a hard knock, should an occasion arise for the owner to descend to that kind of argument.

He was reported, vicariously, to have been 'disappointed with the Atlantic' of which much, including headlines, was made. This first experience of newsmen *en masse* was unnerving, especially since his every word was likely to be reported. However, he rapidly learned the value of the 'sound bite' and doubtless prepared in advance his famous riposte to the customs official: 'I have nothing to declare but my genius.'

Despite the round of receptions and general lionising by New York Society his lecture, 'The English Renaissance', was ready in time for his first appearance on 9 January. It was listened to attentively but it was over-long and over-theoretical. Having become the self-appointed figurehead for a movement he needed a manifesto and had borrowed heavily from Ruskin, Morris and Pater, often verbatim. It was an attempt at some kind of synthesis between the Whistler–Rossetti school of creative art and the more down-to-earth applications of the decorative arts movement as championed by Morris and Ruskin. The subtleties were lost on many in the audience. During his first engagements they were often bored and showed it. Within a month the lecture had undergone a radical transformation to become 'The Decorative Arts' – shorter, simpler and altogether more appealing – which he fine-tuned, adding appropriate anecdotes as he travelled around the country. A second lecture, 'The House Beautiful', reserved for towns in which he

had two engagements, was written during a
week's break from lecturing in Chicago. It reads
in places like a Habitat catalogue of the 1970s:
use plain rather than heavy cut glass; enjoy the
simple beauty of natural wood; and lay down
rush matting if you cannot afford the finest and
most expensive in Persian rugs.

The fifty-lecture tour, originally planned to last
four months eventually stretched to nearly a year,
with a punishing schedule of 140 lectures in 260
days from the east to the west coast and back, and
twice up into Canada. The Press and the audiences
treated him largely with amusement, except on the
rare occasions when he lectured on Ireland to the
Irish who still held his mother in high respect. He
also won praise for his comments on the Phoenix
Park murder of the Chief Secretary for Ireland,
Lord Cavendish, in May: 'When liberty comes with
hands dabbled in blood it is hard to shake hands
with her. We forget how much England is to blame.
She is reaping the fruit of seven centuries of injust-
ice,' he said to the *Philadelphia Press*. He had a surprisingly enthusiastic welcome, too, from the miners of
Leadville, Colorado in the Rockies. Probably
because their cultures were so widely separated, neither prejudged the other, but the fact that Oscar
drank whisky with them glass for glass and publicly
said that he considered them the best-dressed men
in America will have endeared him to them. In
Kentucky, by sheer coincidence, he quoted Keats's

UNION SQUARE THEATRE

OFFICIAL PROGRAMME.

Proprietors and Managers,...................Messrs. SHOOK & COLLIER.

Week Ending August 25th, 1883.

Every Evening at 8.   Saturday Matinee at 2.

MARIE PRESCOTT,
IN
OSCAR WILDE'S
NEW PLAY,

VERA;
Or, THE NIHILIST.

THE PALACE.

THE CZAR	MR GEO. C. BONIFACE
PRIME MINISTER	MR. ED. LAMB
BARON RAFF	MR. JAMES WRIGHT
PRINCE PETROVICH	MR. WM. WILSON
COUNT ROUVALOFF	MR. JOHN F. DE GEZ
MARQUIS DE POIVRARD	MR. CHAS. DAY
GENERAL KOTEMKEN	MR. GEORGE S. PAXTON
COLONEL OF THE GUARD	MR. THOS. BRANICK
PAGE	MR. LEWIS MANN

Body Guard, Soldiers, and Courtiers.

THE PEOPLE.

PETER SAVOUROFF, an Inn-keeper	MR. JULIUS KAHN
DEMITRI, his son	MR. FRED. LOTTO
VERA, his daughter	MARIE PRESCOTT
MICHAEL, a peasant	MR. B. W. TURNER
ALEXIS, a medical student	MR. LEWIS MORRISON
NICHOLAS, a child	FRANKIE FURLONG
PRESIDENT OF THE NIHILISTS	MR. J. R. FURLONG
PROFESSOR MARFA	MR. EDWARD HARDING

Conspirator, Nihilists and Peasant.

FOR REMAINDER OF PROGRAMME, SEE THIRD PAGE.

The Orchestra, under the direction of Mr. Henry Tissington, will perform the
following choice selections :

OVERTURE	"KING MYDAS,"	EILENBERG
WALTZ	"DOLORES,"	WALDTEUFEL
GAVOTTE	"FORGET-ME-NOT "	SIESE
POLONAISE	" FESTIVAL,"	BARTHOLOMAUS
SELECTION	"THE QUEEN'S LACE HANDKERCHIEF,"	STRAUSS

With Solos for Violin, Flute, Clarionet, Cornet, etc.

'Sonnet on Blue' to an audience in which was sitting the poet's niece. She so enjoyed Wilde's lecture that she invited him home to see her uncle's papers and later gave him the manuscript of the sonnet itself.

In between lectures he made time to meet Henry Longfellow, Oliver Wendell Holmes and Walt Whitman. Even more important, he arranged for *Vera* to be staged in New York the following year and was commissioned on the basis of a scenario to write a blank-verse tragedy, *The Duchess of Padua*, for the actress Mary Anderson. The newspapers back home had reported extensively on his tour, even down to the details of when he had had his hair cut, so there was the bonus of having his reputation kept alive in his absence. Overall it had been a resounding success for the amount of exposure he had received; not least, he returned home at the end of December with more than $6000 (£1200) in his pocket.

After a month in London Oscar went to Paris. *The Duchess of Padua* was due to be delivered by the end of March and, despite the attractive prospect he had entertained a year before of whiling away time in Venice, Rome or Athens, Paris was the obvious city in which to write. He spoke the lan-

Willie, the critic, consoles Oscar, the playwright for the failure of *Vera* in New York. Caricature by Alfred Bryan in *The Entre'acte*, 1 September 1883.

Above and opposite
The preacher of 'The House Beautiful' in Birmingham, probably in November 1884 when he was lecturing there. *(Photos Robert W. Thrupp)*

Above **Flyer for Wilde's lecture tour in the English provinces 1883-4 during which he gave as many lectures as on his American tour but was far less well paid.**

guage and there would not be the distractions of friends in London. As it was, he rapidly developed a friendship with a young English journalist, Robert Sherard, which would last way beyond his death: Sherard became Wilde's first and most voluminous biographer, though in his muddle-headed way and spaniel-like devotion, Sherard entirely overlooked his friend's homosexuality before his arrest and misunderstood it thereafter.

Wilde installed himself in the Hôtel Voltaire on the Rive Gauche overlooking the Seine, where he stayed for the next three months. Fresh from preaching the gospel of Aestheticism to material-istic America, he now found himself in the midst of French decadence. There was a world of differ-ence between the rarified and frequently intellec-tual atmosphere of the first, and the overtly exotic promiscuity of the second. He threw himself in a slightly affected way into what he regarded as lit-erary Paris, aping Balzac with his white dressing-gown, the critic Paul Bourget with his ivory cane (who in turn had borrowed from it from Balzac) and Baudelaire in his consumption of alcohol. Through Sherard he met many of the foremost lit-erary figures of the period, among them Edmond de Goncourt, who wrote rather unflatteringly in his diary of Wilde as '*cet individu au sexe douteux, au langage de cabotin, aux récits blagueurs*'. Victor Hugo, by now eighty-one, fell asleep after exchanging some pre-liminary courtesies with Wilde at one of his soirées,

which was a disappointment. Maurice Rollinat came to dine with him at the Hôtel Voltaire and recited from his recently published collection *Les Névroses*, dark and sensual poems which appealed to Wilde in that Rollinat seemed to have taken on the mantle of Baudelaire. There must have been a certain fascination, too, at the autodestructive Rollinat, who was drugging himself to death almost as quickly as Verlaine was poisoning himself with absinthe. These were the *poètes maudits* of whom his experience as yet had only been in the imagination. His meeting with Verlaine in the Café Vachette was less of a success, Wilde finding his appearance off-putting and Verlaine annoyed that his empty glass was not refilled by the younger man paying court to him. In Wilde's case, Verlaine's own stormy relationship with Rimbaud – whom he shot at and wounded in 1873, earning himself two years in prison – was to be repeated under different circumstances but with far more disastrous consequences.

The Duchess of Padua was duly sent off to Mary Anderson at the end of March. In the event she turned it down, which was as much a blow to his finances as it was to his ego. He had had an advance of $1000, but he had been expecting another $4000 on acceptance and living off the expectation. 'We shan't be able to dine with the Duchess tonight, Robert,' he remarked when the telegram arrived. *The Duchess* was eventually performed in New York in 1893 to as bad a reception as *Vera* had suffered a decade before.

Left James Whistler, some of whose theories on art Wilde 'borrowed' for his own lectures, and whose friendship Wilde enjoyed from 1879 to 1886 when they came to verbal blows. The response 'You will, Oscar, you will,' to Wilde's 'I wish I'd said that,' is attributed to him.

Opposite **Oil portrait of Oscar Wilde painted in 1883 by American Artist Harper Pennington,** sometime pupil of James Whistler.

The stay in Paris, however, had laid the foundations of the francophilia which remained with him until the end of his life and which, by strange irony, was to some degree responsible for his catastrophic downfall. He remained for another month, productive only in that he confirmed a few friendships for the future, especially that of Sarah Bernhardt, whom he would later invite to play the lead in *Salomé*. His American resources were fast dwindling and since his somewhat tenuous new asset was his reputation as a lecturer, he returned to England to make the most of it.

If his transatlantic trial by fire had given him money and experience, it had also given him a lifelong supply of gentle jibes at the Americans and he was able to supplement his existing lecture on 'The House Beautiful' with 'Personal Impressions of America'. Colonel Morse, who had organised the American lectures, now arranged a British tour for Oscar and although the fees did not match up to what the Americans had paid, at least he had income to offset his spending. It was on a lecture visit to Dublin in November 1883 that he proposed to Constance Lloyd.

Constance was four years younger than Oscar and the daughter of a prominent Irish barrister who had died when she was sixteen. Since her mother, with whom she did not get on, had remarried, Constance had been living in London with her grandfather. Oscar had first met her some time in

Dec. 1883

To clean Arthur from his friend Wilde

Oscar in 1889 by the Cameron Studio run by Julia Margaret Cameron's son, H. H. H. Cameron, who was strongly influenced by his mother's style of portraiture (see also pp 121 and 123). Arthur Fish, to whom the photo is inscribed, was Oscar's deputy when he was editing *The Woman's World*.

the early summer of 1881 through Dublin friends and had immediately taken a strong liking to her. The feeling was reciprocal and from the defensive way she wrote to her brother Otho, it took her no time at all to find her way behind the aesthetic pose.

> I can't help liking him, because when he's talking to me alone he's never a bit affected, and speaks naturally, excepting that he uses better language than most people. Grandpa, I think, likes Oscar, but of course the others laugh at him, because they don't choose to see anything but that he wears long hair and looks aesthetic.

Constance herself was well-read, spoke several European languages and had an independent mind which she had no hesitation in speaking. She was also beautiful. There had been some mild flirtation at social occasions on Oscar's return from Paris but nothing to suppose that he would ask her to marry him. 'Prepare yourself for an astounding piece of news,' she wrote to Otho. 'I am engaged to Oscar Wilde and perfectly and insanely happy.' Oscar, equally, seemed to be walking on air: 'We are, of course, desperately in love,' he wrote to his sculptor friend Waldo Story. 'I have been obliged to be away nearly all the time since our engagement, civilising the provinces by my remarkable lectures, but we telegraph to each other twice a day, and the telegraph clerks have become quite romantic in consequence.'

It has been conjectured, occasionally, that Oscar only married Constance in order to quell rumours about his possible homosexuality, as well as to provide him with a regular income. Certainly his financial state was far from good, but the £250 annual income from Constance's marriage settlement (it became £800 after her grandfather's death) was no fortune and had it been entirely a marriage of convenience he could have done much better for himself elsewhere. Whether or not he was genuinely in love with her seems idle speculation; no one but a cynic could read the sole surviving letter he wrote to her from Edinburgh six months after the wedding and still maintain that the marriage was a sham:

> Dear and Beloved, Here am I, and you at the Antipodes. O execrable facts that keep our lips from kissing though our souls are one. What can I tell you by letter? Alas nothing that I would tell you. The messages of the gods to each other travel not by pen and ink and indeed your bodily presence here would not make you more real: for I feel your fingers in my hair, and your cheek brushing mine. The air is full of the music of your voice, my body and soul no longer seem mine, but mingled in some exquisite ecstasy with yours. I feel incomplete without you. Ever and ever yours, Oscar.

Above **Constance Lloyd around the time of her marriage to Oscar in 1884: 'a grave, slight, violet-eyed little Artemis, with great coils of heavy brown hair,' as Oscar described her to Lillie Langtry.** *(Photo W. & D. Downey, London)*

Below **Constance in 1892, now married to an aesthete and mother of two.** *(Photo Kingsbury & Notcutt, London)*

Above **Constance's wedding ring, designed by Oscar to split in two halves around the circumference while still remaining linked. Their names and the marriage date 29 May 1884 are engraved inside.**

Opposite **Constance Wilde about 1887.**

Below **Constance in 1892 at the time *Lady Windermere's Fan* was first staged.** *(Photo Kingsbury & Notcutt, London)*

The wedding took place on 29 May 1884, followed by a honeymoon in Paris and Dieppe. By the end of June they were back in London. They had taken a lease on a house in Tite Street, a few doors from where Oscar had lived with Frank Miles three years before, and London was waiting to see what the 'Professor of Aesthetics' would do with his own House Beautiful. The interior redecorating took an interminable time due to legal disputes with the contractors and it was not until early the following year that husband and wife could move in. Constance was already three months pregnant.

Oscar's main concern was to avoid pre-Raphaelite excess as well as the ponderous style of the period. For example, my father, Vyvyan, remembered that:

> The prevailing note in the dining room was white blending with pale blue and yellow. The walls were white; the Chippendale chairs were painted white and upholstered in white plush, and the carpet, concerning the cleanliness of which we were constantly being admonished, was also white. Nursery meals were also served in the dining room, unless my mother was giving a luncheon party, because the nursery itself was so far away from the kitchen.

It was a thoroughly impractical décor for a house with two small children in the centre of grime-laden Victorian London, but the lecturer who

Constance at the time Oscar's affair with Lord Alfred Douglas began. 'She could not understand me and I was bored to death with married life. But she had some sweet points in her character and was wonderfully loyal to me.' *(Photo Kingsbury & Notcutt, London)*

'civilised the provinces' with his views on the House Beautiful had little choice but to follow his own precepts. And the two children arrived in quick succession, Cyril in 1885, and Vyvyan in 1886.

By now Wilde was thirty-two. He had a family to support, no regular income, he was lecturing sporadically, but even with two new subjects, 'The Value of Art in Modern Life' and 'Dress', there was a limit to how often he could visit the main provincial cities. The aesthetic notoriety had begun to look a trifle threadbare; *Punch*, which had satirised him fifty times in 1881–2, ignored him completely in 1886. On various occasions since leaving Oxford he had applied, like Matthew Arnold before him, to become an Inspector of Schools, the latest attempt being in February 1886 through his old tutor, Mahaffy. There might perhaps have been renewed pressure from his mother who, on his engagement, had written a little uncharacteristically: 'I would like you to have a small house in London and live the literary life and teach Constance to correct proofs and eventually go into Parliament.' He

Cyril and Vyvyan as 'Bubbles' and 'Little Lord Fauntleroy'. One day in Tite Street they protested at being paraded by their father in this way before his guests and stripped stark naked before prancing into the drawing-room.

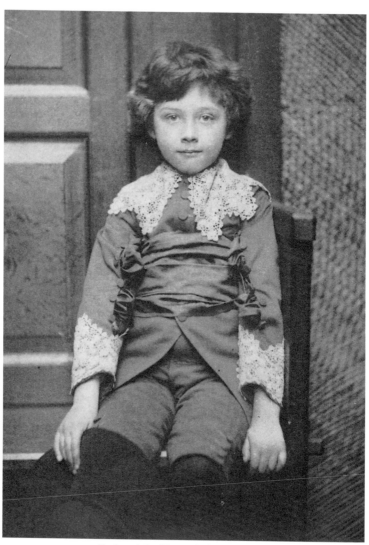

Cyril aged six. *(Photo Frederick Hollyer, London)*

Vyvyan Wilde about 1891 aged five. *(Photo William Salomon, Reading)*

Cyril and Vyvyan Wilde in 'aesthetic' children's dress which they hated,
preferring sailor suits. *(see opposite)*

even shares some of his concerns with a hopeful young author who had written to him for advice:

> As regards your prospects in literature, believe me that it is impossible to live by literature. By journalism a man may make an income, but rarely by pure literary work. I would strongly advise you to try and make some profession, such as that of tutor, the basis and mainstay of your life, and to keep literature for your finest, rarest moments. Remember that London is full of young men working for literary success, and that you must carve your way to fame. Laurels don't come for the asking.

Then, as he hovered dangerously on the edge of respectability at the beginning of 1887, his life changed. Not dramatically at first, but through the cumulative effect of several unconnected events. When Oscar had married Constance she had been slim and graceful, with a boyish figure even, and a slightly gamine look about her. It was a type which unquestionably attracted him. Aimée Lowther, a girl of similar build, recounted how Oscar had once said to her around that time, 'Aimée, Aimée, if you had been a boy you'd have wrecked my life.' Two years of almost continual pregnancy had taken its toll on Constance's body as Oscar later confided to his friend Frank Harris: 'When I married, my wife was a beautiful girl, white and slim as a lily with

Above **Vyvyan in his favourite sailor suit.** He remembered it 60 years on: 'Not an ordinary children's sailor suit either but a suit made of real naval cloth by a naval tailor with a black silk scarf and a knife at the end of a lanyard.' (Photo The Cameron Studio)

Below **Cyril aged seven at Cromer, Norfolk, presumably taken when his father was there working on** *A Woman of No Importance* in August 1892. (Photo H. Mace)

121

Above **A post-aesthetic Oscar in about 1887.**
(Photo Debenham & Gould, Bournemouth)

Below **The only surviving letter from Oscar to Constance, written when he was lecturing in Edinburgh at the end of 1884.**

dancing eyes and gay rippling laughter like music. In a year or so all the flowerlike grace had vanished; she became heavy, shapeless, deformed.' Although Harris is not known for his reliability, this has the ring of truth about it. And it was not only motherhood which Constance had to contend with; Oscar still needed constant intellectual stimulus which as a bachelor he had found easily enough among the literary and artistic circles he frequented. Now the ties of marriage made it less easy to do so spontaneously. Marriage undeniably had its social advantages, nonetheless the duties of a husband and father, the necessity to make money and, despite her intelligence, the limited intellectual companionship which Constance was able to afford him, put his feet rather too firmly on the ground for one who had spent most of his life flying.

It was in the spring of 1887, too, that the reviewing which Wilde had been doing, largely for the *Pall Mall Gazette*, suddenly bore fruit. On the whole, his pieces were far more carefully thought out than the job required and it was partly through them that he had come to the attention of Thomas Wemyss Reid, the general manager of Cassell's. Reid had started a magazine called *The Lady's World* in November 1886 which had been much less successful than the publishers had expected. He approached Wilde to revitalise it. For Wilde it was a perfect opportunity to put himself back in the public eye, as well as giving him an official calling

card. He replied: 'It seems to me that at present it is too feminine and not sufficiently womanly . . . we should take a wider range, as well as a high standpoint, and deal not merely with what women wear but with what they think, and what they feel.' He also suggested that Cassell's change the name to *The Woman's World* which, with some reluctance, they did. He spent the spring and summer preparing new editorial ground along the lines he had proposed and started as editor in November. He would travel from Sloane Square to Charing Cross by the underground and walk the rest of the way to Ludgate Hill, though the idea of Oscar Wilde as an early urban commuter appears faintly ludicrous. At any rate he soon tired of the monotony that a regular job required of him and left in October 1889. Not long before, he was asked how often he went into the office. 'I used to go three times a week for an hour a day,' he replied, 'but I have since struck off one of the days.' Wilde's time at *The Woman's World* is sometimes regarded by his biographers as an interesting but unimportant interlude in his writing life. It was more than that: it re-established him as a front-line writer; it relieved the acute financial pressures; and above all it gave him some of those 'finest, rarest moments' for 'literature', effectively kick-starting him into the great creative years of his life.

Above and Opposite
Oscar in the year that he started work on *Dorian Gray*, 1889. In a letter he admitted certain autobiographical elements in the novel: 'Basil Hallward is what I think I am; Lord Henry is what the world thinks me; Dorian is what I would like to be – in other ages perhaps.' It was as well that Edward Carson did not have access to this letter during the libel trial. (*Photos W. & D. Downey, London*)

Robert Ross about 24 as Wilde would have known him in the early 1890s. He remained a close friend until Wilde's death and later became his literary executor.

The last and perhaps the most significant event of 1887 was the arrival in his life of a young man, Robert Ross. In that year Ross came to stay with the Wildes in Tite Street as a paying guest and is generally thought to have been Wilde's first homosexual lover; indeed, Oscar admitted as much to another friend, Reggie Turner, on his deathbed. Later Robbie denied that he had been Wilde's lover but said that he 'wouldn't have minded' if he had been. Certainly, his loyalty when the crash came, his devoted friendship during Oscar's imprisonment and last years in exile, as well as his astute and self-less management of the Wilde literary estate for the two boys after his death, all make it seem likely. This discovery in himself of a different sexuality, that he may previously have felt but had been reluctant or unable to indulge, could now be given expression. It was, however, a dangerous indulgence, for in 1885 the Criminal Law Amendment Act had been passed under which same-sex relations between men (but not women) were punished by imprisonment. But there was a Faustian thirst for experience in Wilde which needed to be satisfied. Only a year before he had written to a young undergraduate friend at Cambridge:

> I myself would sacrifice everything for a new experience and know that there is no such thing as a new experience at all. . . . I would

go to the stake for a sensation and be a sceptic to the last. . . . There is an unknown land full of strange flowers and subtle perfumes, a land of which it is a joy of all joys to dream, a land where all things are perfect and poisonous.

Over the next two years Wilde's childhood Ireland spilled out on to paper – 'a Celtic world dominated by ghosts and God' as one of his compatriots has described it. Folklore, superstition and the supernatural fill 'The Canterville Ghost', 'Lord Arthur Savile's Crime' and his first collection of children's stories, *The Happy Prince and Other Tales*. He hated the idea, incidentally, that they were to be for children at all and referred to them as 'written, not for children but for childlike people from eighteen to eighty'. The paranormal held a constant fascination for Wilde, and not just as an object of literary study. Like Lord Arthur Savile, Wilde had his palm read. In 1893 he was told by Count Louis Hamon that his left hand promised brilliant success while the right showed impending ruin. 'The left hand is the hand of a king but the right that of a king who will send himself into exile.' While he was half-way through his prison sentence his mother died. On the night of her death, as he later recounted to a friend, Vincent O'Sullivan, she appeared to him in his cell dressed for out-of-doors. He asked her to stay a while, take off her cloak and sit down but she shook her head sadly, refused and then vanished. When his wife came to break the news to him a few days later he simply

Above and Opposite
'People nowadays are so absolutely superficial that they don't understand the philosophy of the superficial. . . . Sentiment is all very well for the buttonhole. But the essential thing for a necktie is style. A well-tied tie is the first serious step in life.' Oscar in 1892. *(Photos Ellis & Walery, London)*

127

said, 'Yes, I knew it already.' After his release from prison he went to another palmist in Paris. 'I am puzzled,' she said. 'By your line of life you died two years ago. I cannot explain the fact except by supposing that since then you have been living on the line of your imagination.' Once he was invited to dine with the 'Thirteen Club' whose sole aim was to defy popular superstition and who arranged dinners of thirteen courses with thirteen guests at thirteen tables after which they smashed mirrors. He replied saying that he could not possibly dine with a society with so wicked an object as theirs. 'I love superstitions. They are the colour element of thought and imagination. They are the opponents of common sense. Common sense is the enemy of romance. Leave us some unreality. Do not make us too offensively sane.'

It was this element of offensive sanity to which Wilde next turned his attention in 1889 in his essay 'The Decay of Lying' in which he made a plea for more imagination, more invention to counteract the growing influence of excessive realism in literature. 'I have blown my trumpet against the gate of dullness,' he wrote at the time it was published. It was his first act of open defiance against the literary establishment; the very title alone was designed to give high-minded Victorians apoplexy.

> The ancient historians gave us delightful fiction in the form of fact; the modern novelist presents us with dull facts under the guise of fiction. Many a young man starts in life with a

Oil portrait of Constance Lloyd in 1882 by Louis Desange.

Top left **Thomas de Witt Talmage**, a Presbyterian preacher who was drawing vast crowds, is worried about the success of his rival. Top right 'The name of Dante Gabriel Rossetti is heard for the first time in the Western States of America.' Watercolour by Max Beerbohm.

Caricature from *The Judge*, September 1883, contrasting Wilde's financially successful lecture tour the year before with the failure of *Vera*.

THE JUDGE

A THING OF BEAUTY NOT A JOY FOREVER.
Rise and Fall of a "Vera" Wilde Æsthete.

A practical aspect for the doctrine of Aesthetics. Oscar promotes Madame Fontaine's Bosom Beautifier. 'Just as sure as the sun will rise tomorrow, just so sure will it enlarge and beautify the bosom,' it boasted.

Top left **Robert Ross**, the most loyal and devoted of all Wilde's friends and later his literary executor. Pastel drawing by William Rothenstein in 1899.

Above **Aubrey Beardsley** painted by Jacques-Emile Blanche in 1895.

Left **Edward Carson** who defended the Marquis of Queensberry against Wilde's charge of criminal libel. Caricature by 'Lib' (Liberio Prosperi) in *Vanity Fair*, 3 November 1893. Wilde and Carson had been contemporaries at Trinity College and when Oscar heard that he had taken the case, he is said to have remarked: 'No doubt he will perform his task with all the added bitterness of an old friend.'

Opposite **Chalk and pastel drawing of Douglas** in 1893 by William Rothenstein.

THE SPHINX BY OSCAR WILDE

MEL
AN
CHO
LIA

WITH DECORATIONS BY CHARLES RICKETTS
LONDON MDCCCXCIV
ELKIN MATHEWS AND JOHN LANE . AT THE SIGN OF THE BODLEY HEAD.

Title page for Wilde's poem *The Sphinx* designed by Charles Ricketts and published in 1894.

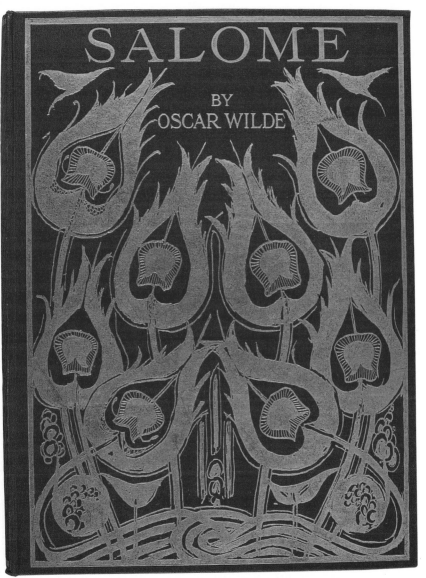

Beardsley's original cover design for *Salomé* which was not used until 1906.

Speranza after the death of Sir William, probably some time in the mid-1880s. Coloured ambrotype.

natural gift for exaggeration, which if nurtured in sympathetic surroundings, might grow into something really great and wonderful. But in a short time he develops a morbid and unhealthy faculty of truth-telling and often ends up by writing novels which are so life-like that no one can possibly believe in their probability.

He seized in particular on a highly popular novel, *Robert Elsmere*, of which he said that it was 'a master-piece of the *genre ennuyeux*. Indeed it is only in England that such a book could be produced. England is the home of lost ideas.' It was doubtless at the back of Lady Bracknell's mind, too, when she described Miss Prism's abandoned literary endeavour as 'a three-volume novel of more than usually revolting sentimentality'. But if 'The Decay of Lying' essay raised a few eyebrows, the publication of *The Picture of Dorian Gray* was to become the practical application of those views and overnight drew up the battle lines between Wilde and the world of Victorian literature.

That autumn the publisher J. M. Stoddart, an acquaintance from Wilde's lecture tour in America with whom he had visited Walt Whitman, arrived in London and invited him to dinner. Stoddart was in town to promote *Lippincott's Magazine* and to solicit stories from English authors. Wilde initially seems to have offered him 'The Fisherman and His Soul' one of the stories that later appeared in his second collection of fairy stories *A House of Pomegranates*. Stoddart turned it down as being too

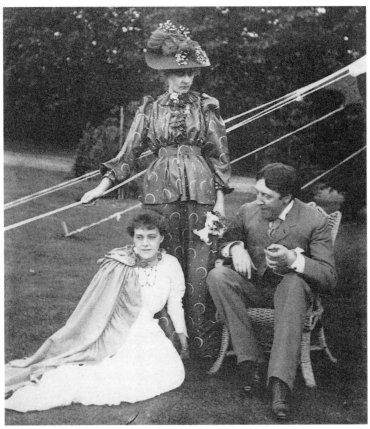

Opposite top **Jean and Walter Palmer** profited from the family's biscuit fortune to hold regular literary and artistic gatherings at their house near Reading. It was there that Oscar Wilde and George Meredith first met. Here, Constance, also present, is seated on the left. Jean Palmer is seated behind Oscar and her husband Walter is standing far left.

Opposite bottom **Same as above – more informal poses.**

Above **Jean Palmer** seated on the ground. Constance looks bored holding her husband's trademark lily and listening to familiar repartee.

House party at the Palmers in Reading, September 1892. Front l. to r. David Bispham, George Meredith, Jean Palmer, H. B. Irving. Back l. to r. Louise Jopling, Wilde, unknown, Marie Meredith, Johnston Forbes-Robertson, unknown.

short and unsuitable for an adult audience, so Wilde wrote *Dorian Gray* for him instead.

It is not known whether Wilde had already written and submitted 'The Fisherman and His Soul' to Stoddart by this stage, or had simply recounted it to him in the inimitable way he had of creating stories out of thin air and to which all who ever heard him do so have testified. What is important is that it was a current idea with which he was playing. The fisherman falls in love with a mermaid and sells his soul to consummate his love for her. Dorian Gray offers his soul to remain in love with himself and his youth. The fisherman abandons his love for a life of evil, but repents and is reunited with his soul in death. For Dorian death does not reunite him with a redeeming soul. His is not a high-minded renunciation of his evil life, simply the desire to be free of his conscience, and with the final destruction of his portrait he achieves merely the opposite, tying himself eternally to his loathsome double. The motives and the outcome have become sinister. Divine forgiveness for the renunciation of evil no longer seems to have a place in Oscar's world. It has become a Greek rather than a Christian view of destiny. From the redemptive qualities which allow young Virginia to lay the Canterville ghost's soul to rest and the deeply Christian, almost parable-like 'Selfish Giant' and 'The Happy Prince', he has progressed through the cynical 'Nightingale and the Rose' to the dark and disturbing conclusions in *Dorian Gray* and 'The

Fisherman and His Soul' where the concept of beauty has become associated with temptation, danger and death. It was a tormented period in Wilde's life. Still married, he had become aware of both his homosexuality and of the need, at that stage at least, to conceal it. The concealment of the double life later became the theme of all his four major plays.

Dorian Gray was published in the July 1890 number of *Lippincott's*. The press response was astounding. The *Scots Observer* wrote:

> The story – which deals with matters only fit for the Criminal Investigation Department or a hearing *in camera* – is discreditable alike to author and editor. Mr Wilde has brains, art and style; but if he can write for none but outlawed noblemen and perverted telegraph boys, the sooner he takes to tailoring (or some other decent trade) the better for his own reputation and the public morals.

The 'outlawed noblemen and perverted telegraph boys' was an oblique reference to the so-called Cleveland Street scandal of August the year before in which a house had been raided where young men were found to be offering their services to aristocratic customers. The Government brought pressure to bear on the police not to make arrests until the influential clients of the establishment had been able to cover their tracks. Public opinion about this unmentionable vice was running high.

Even for Oscar, who had been conducting his own public-relations campaign off and on since leaving Oxford, the effect must have been surprising. Today an author's agent would count the column inches of vituperation engendered by a such a story, declare that all publicity was good publicity

Oscar at work on *Salomé* as seen by Aubrey Beardsley in 1892.

OSCAR WILDE AT WORK

"(IL NE PAUT PAS LE REGARDER)"

FRENCH DICTH

AHN'S FIRST COURS

DORIAN GRAY

GAUTIER

FAMILY BIBLE

TROIS CONTES

SWINBURNE

FRENCH VERBS AT A GLANCE

PARALLEL.

Joe, the Fat Boy in Pickwick, startles the Old Lady; Oscar, the Fad Boy in Lippincott's, startles Mrs. Grundy.

Oscar, the Fad Boy. " I want to make your flesh creep ! "

Above **Oscar Wilde 'Among the Audience'** by Alfred Bryan in the *Illustrated Sporting and Dramatic News,* 9 April 1992. The other figure is his brother Willie.

Left Oscar presents a shocked and prudish Mrs Grundy with a copy of *Dorian Gray.* Cartoon by E.T. Reed, *Punch,* 19 July 1890.

and sell the author's next book for a six-figure sum. But Victorian London simply squirmed with discomfort. Constance was said to have remarked: 'Since Oscar wrote *Dorian Gray,* no one will speak to us.'

Dorian Gray has been described as the only French novel ever written in English and it was unquestionably Wilde's fascination with the French *décadents* which partly inspired it. When the British went to *fin de siècle* Paris to take their fleshly pleasures, whatever they found there they left behind. Wilde had been going there regularly since

Below **Wilde, anticipating the Lord Chamberlain's decision on *Salomé* threatened to emigrate to France. He was portrayed by Bernard Partridge in *Punch* on 9 July 1892 as a conscript in the French army.**

137

the mid-1880s for the experience of a completely different culture, but he committed
the unpardonable offence of bringing it
home in his suitcase and putting it into
print. Late in 1891 he went back to immerse
himself again, this time to write a radically
new play and to write it in French. Six
months later Sarah Bernhardt had been persuaded to take the title role in *Salomé* and
had started rehearsals in London, when the Lord
Chamberlain, then the censor of plays, refused it a
licence. Wilde was incensed but the stench of decadence was overpowering for English nostrils. It
simply wasn't playing the game and it wasn't the
stuff that Empire builders were made of. *Dorian
Gray* had been bad enough, but sexual deviance,
necrophilia and blasphemy all rolled into one was
intolerable.

In the meantime Nature, as Oscar would
always have it, imitated Art and into his life
stepped his nemesis, his own Dorian Gray in
the form of Lord Alfred 'Bosie' Douglas,
third son of the Marquis of Queensberry.
They were introduced some time in the
summer of 1891 by the poet Lionel
Johnson. Bosie having read *Dorian Gray*, as he
said, nine times, already knew of Oscar.
Wilde at the time was thirty-seven and
Douglas twenty-one. Douglas was an undergraduate at Oxford, gifted with decided

poetic talents, as well as exceptional good looks. They met occasionally as acquaintances during the next year until Douglas came to Wilde for help over an indiscreet letter with which he was being blackmailed. Soon after, they must have become

Above **Caricature of Wilde in top hat by Beatrice Whistler.**

Right **On the first night of** *Lady Windermere's Fan* **Wilde made an amusing and outrageous curtain speech smoking a cigarette. The critics and cartoonists took him to task – here Bernard Partridge,** *Punch,* **5 March 1892.**

FANCY PORTRAIT.

QUITE TOO-TOO PUFFICKLY PRECIOUS!!

Being Lady Windy-mère's Fan-cy Portrait of the new dramatic author,
Shakspeare Sheridan Oscar Puff, Esq.

["He addressed from the stage a public audience, mostly composed of ladies, pressing between his daintily-gloved fingers a still burning and half-smoked cigarette."—*Daily Telegraph.*]

lovers and on Wilde's side the friendship with Douglas rapidly turned into an infatuation and he made no secret of his feelings, asking Douglas out to dine with him continually, sending him letters, telegrams and gifts of every description. Douglas in turn became captivated by Wilde's charm and the magical quality of his conversation, and from then until Wilde's arrest three years later they were in each other's company as much as possible.

141

Left The 'Author's Edition' of *Poems* 1892. In reality it was just the unsold copies of the 1882 edition revamped with a new title page by Charles Ricketts and signed by Wilde.

Right John Gray, poet, dramatist and later Catholic priest who came into Wilde's life in 1889, probably as a lover, until replaced in 1892 by Bosie Douglas.

Left John Gray. Lithograph by Raymond Savage.

Below The Ricketts and Shannon design for the title page of *A House of Pomegranates* published in 1891.

Oscar Wilde by William Rothenstein about 1894.

William Rothenstein (left) and Max Beerbohm as undergraduates at Oxford. Oscar said of Max that the gods had bestowed on him the gift of perpetual old age.

Bosie was no innocent when he met Oscar; far from it. He was already at home in the homosexual underworld whereas Oscar, apart from Robbie Ross and possibly John Gray, seemed to have been limiting himself to the idea rather than the practice. He enjoyed being surrounded by intelligent, good-looking young men but the sexual encounters, from all we can gather, were occasional and harmless. In a letter written while Wilde was in prison Douglas said: 'People look upon me as the victim of his superior age and wisdom. . . . All this is so utterly wide of the real truth. So far from his leading me astray it was I that (unwittingly) pushed him over the precipice.' Bosie introduced him to the *demi-monde* of the 'renter', the male prostitute, and Oscar was fascinated by what he found.

> People thought it dreadful of me to
> have entertained at dinner the evil
> things of life, and to have found
> pleasure in their company. But they,
> from the point of view through which
> I, as an artist in life, approached them,
> were delightfully suggestive and
> stimulating. It was like feasting with
> panthers. The danger was half the
> excitement. . . . They were to me the
> brightest of gilded snakes. Their
> poison was part of their perfection.

144

It had been difficult to make ends meet financially before Oscar met Bosie; thereafter it was quite impossible. *Dorian Gray* had enjoyed a *succès de scandale* and had been expanded and published as a book but it had made little money. It was fortunate, therefore, that the actor-manager George Alexander had commissioned Wilde to write a play when he took over the St James's Theatre late in 1890. Wilde remained uninspired until the following summer when he started work on *Lady Windermere's Fan.* By October it was complete and it opened in February 1892. It was novel, it was effective theatre and with the public it was a triumph. He seemed at last to have found his true literary medium and lost little time in writing *A Woman of No Importance* (1892), *An Ideal Husband* (1893) and *The Importance of Being Earnest* (1894), all along broadly similar lines. It was a logical conclusion that this master of conversation should burst the constraints of prose and finish up nightly addressing the largest drawing-room in London – the West End stage. It also made him many 'bags of red and yellow gold' as he put it – *Lady Windermere* bringing in £7000, apparently, in its first year. The other plays made less, especially the last two which were taken off at the time of his arrest, but it was a sobering thought for Wilde as he sat in Reading Gaol, bankrupted by Queensberry for his court costs, that more than £5000 had been spent in three years on his disastrously extravagant life-style with Bosie Douglas.

'The little note of individualism that makes dress delightful can only be attained nowadays by the colour and treatment of the flower that one wears.' Oscar in 1892.
(Photos Ellis & Wallery, London)

Above **Drawing of Alfred Douglas in November 1895 by William Spindler.**

Below **Lord Alfred Douglas at Oxford in 1891 aged 21.** *(Photo by Gillman & Co.)*

Above **Oscar and Bosie at Oxford probably taken in May 1893 when Douglas was in his last year and Wilde went up on a long visit.** *(Photo by Gillman & Co.)*

Right **Drawing of Douglas by Max Beerbohm in 1891 when they were both undergraduates at Oxford.**

Douglas aged 23. 'Your slim gilt soul walks between passion and poetry. I know Hyacinthus, whom Apollo loved so madly, was you in Greek days,' Wilde wrote to him around that time. *(Photo The Cameron Studio)*

During those three years Wilde maintained, 'my life, as long as you were by my side, was entirely sterile and uncreative'. Bosie later disputed this hotly and asked the world to believe that he had been Oscar's muse. Incentive to make money, perhaps, but muse, no, as any modern chronology of their two lives would show. But if the relationship swung between the sublime and the exasperating for Oscar, it was intolerable for Bosie's father, the 'screaming, scarlet'

Below and Opposite **Bosie was at Oscar's old college, Magdalen, and also read Classics. Unlike Wilde he did no work, despite Oscar's attempts to tutor him, and went down, shortly after these photographs were taken, without a degree.** *(Photos by Gillman & Co.)*

Marquis, who already suspected his eldest son, Viscount Drumlanrig of conducting a homosexual affair with the Foreign Secretary, Lord Rosebery. Queensberry was a mentally unbalanced, arrogant and ill-tempered man who, in private, beat his wife and took no interest in his children. In his public life he is remembered only as the author of the Queensberry rules for boxing. A copy of one of Wilde's letters to Douglas fell into the Marquis's hands, in which he had written 'it is a marvel that those red rose-leaf lips of yours should have been made no less for music of song than for madness of kisses'. He now began to object in the strongest possible terms to his son's association with Wilde and threatened to cut Bosie's allowance if it did not cease immediately. When Douglas refused, Queensberry flew into a frenzy and followed the two of them around the

various hotels and restaurants which they frequented in London, threatening to cause a public scandal if he found them together. In June 1894 Queensberry eventually turned up at Wilde's Tite Street house, bringing with him a prize-fighter, and although he did not accuse Wilde directly of engaging in improper conduct with his son, he said 'you look it and you pose as it, which is just as bad' and swore that he would thrash Wilde if ever he found him again in a public restaurant with Bosie. Wilde's famous reply to this threat was: 'I do not know what the Queensberry rules are, but the Oscar Wilde rule is to shoot on sight.' He showed Queensberry to the door, instructed his manservant never to allow the Marquis to enter his home again and from then on Douglas and Wilde made a point of being seen together in as many public places as possible. Then, in October, Queensberry's heir, Drumlanrig, was killed in what was reported as a shooting accident but believed by those in the know to have been suicide. There was suspicion that he was being blackmailed for his relationship with Rosebery, who by now had become Prime Minister. Queensberry, having lost one son to what he saw as the evils of homosexuality, was determined not to let the matter of Oscar and Bosie rest, and planned to create a disturbance at the

Above **Oscar and Bosie at Cromer in Norfolk, September 1892, where Wilde was writing** *A Woman of No Importance* .

Opposite **Lord Alfred Douglas (in bow tie) with his elder brother, Francis, Viscount Drumlanrig who was widely rumoured to be conducting an affair with Lord Rosebery, Foreign Secretary and later Prime Minister.**

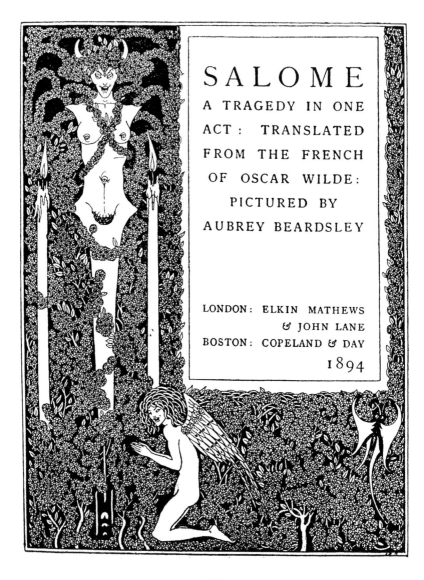

SALOME

A TRAGEDY IN ONE
ACT : TRANSLATED
FROM THE FRENCH
OF OSCAR WILDE :
PICTURED BY
AUBREY BEARDSLEY

LONDON : ELKIN MATHEWS
& JOHN LANE
BOSTON : COPELAND & DAY
1894

Opposite **The title page for the English edition of** *Salomé* **as bowdlerised by the** publisher. Above Aubrey Beardsley's original design showing the genitals of the two figures which were only restored in the 1906 edition.

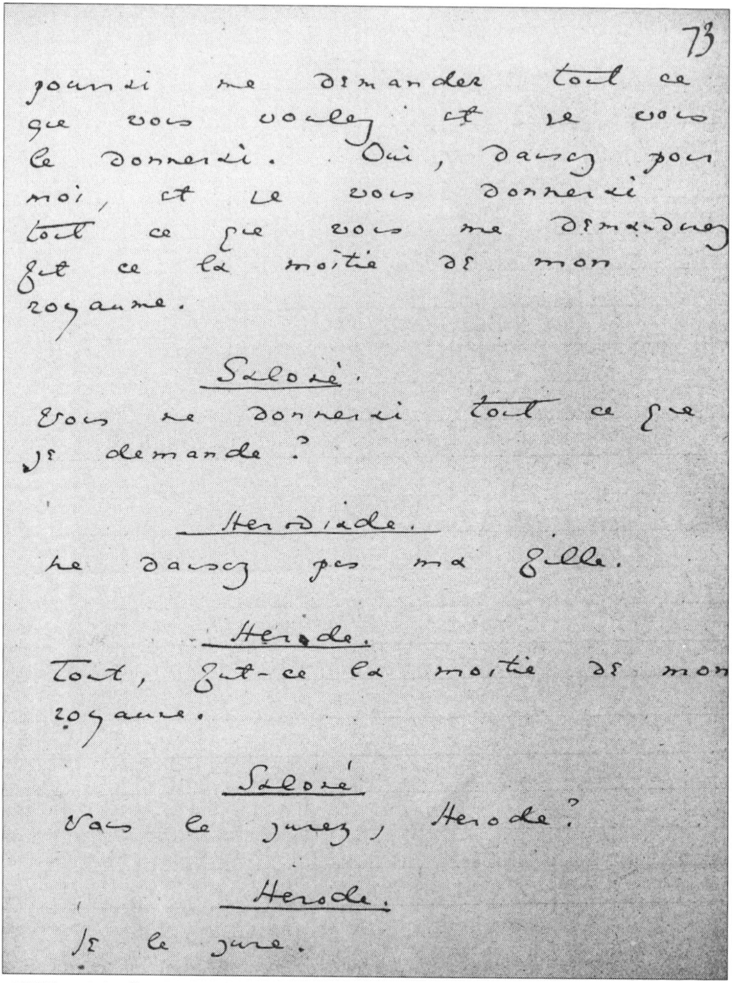

pour si me demander tout ce
que vous voulez et je vous
le donnerai. Oui, dancez pour
moi, et je vous donnerai
tout ce que vous me demandez
fut ce la moitié de mon
royaume.

<u>Salomé.</u>
Vous me donnerai tout ce que
je demande?

<u>Hérodiade.</u>
ne dancez pas ma fille.

<u>Hérode.</u>
Tout, fut-ce la moitié de mon
royaume.

<u>Salomé</u>
Vous le jurez, Hérode?

<u>Hérode.</u>
Je le jure.

Wilde originally wrote *Salomé* in French for performance in French and asked Douglas to translate it for the English edition. The result was not a success. Wilde later wrote of 'the schoolboy faults of your attempted translation'. On this page of the original MS Herod offers Salomé half his kingdom to dance but Wilde makes a couple of grammatical howlers.

154

'Enter Herodias'. The youth on the right was originally naked but the publisher insisted on a fig leaf. Wilde was said to have been unhappy at his own caricature in the bottom corner.

Oscar as a voluptuary from *Pick-Me-Up*, 14 July 1894: 'To rise, to take a little opium, to sleep till lunch, and after again to take a little opium and sleep till dinner, that is a life of pleasure!'

Left and Above **Bosie** photographed in Cairo in the winter of 1893–4. He had been sent there by his mother at Oscar's suggestion. 'His life seems to me aimless, unhappy and absurd.'

Above **Aubrey Beardsley** in the early 1890s.

Left **André Gide** whom Wilde first met in Paris while writing *Salomé* in 1891 and who fell rapidly under Wilde's spell.

Above **Frank Harris**, journalist and writer, in many ways a scoundrel but a loyal and generous friend to Wilde after prison.

AN IDEAL HUSBAND

OSCAR WILDE HAY-MARK-ET THE.AT.RE

Oscar seen as the Ideal Husband by cartoonist Harry Furniss in *Lika Joko*, 12 January 1894.

opening night of *The Importance of Being Earnest* with a grotesque bouquet of vegetables. Wilde, tipped off by a friend, alerted the police and the Marquis was denied entry. A few days later, on 18 February 1895, Queensberry left his card at Wilde's club on which he had written 'For Oscar Wilde posing somdomite [*sic*]'.

At the time Wilde had two plays, *The Importance of Being Earnest* and *An Ideal Husband*, running simultaneously in London's West End. He was successful, he had a substantial income from the theatre receipts and he was much talked about. He was also besotted with his 'golden-haired boy', who loathed his father with a passion and saw an opportunity through Wilde to have him put in the dock, if not in prison. Oscar, as he later said in his long prison letter to Bosie, *De Profundis*, lost his head and sued for criminal libel. 'I was no longer the Captain of my Soul and did not know it. I allowed you to dominate me and your father to frighten me. My judgement forsook me. I saw no possible escape from either of you. Blindly I staggered as an ox into the shambles.' But there is no simple explanation for his conduct. Arrogance born of social and literary success and the belief that he was in some way immune from the Law unquestionably played a part, as did a desire to please young Douglas. There was, too, a perverse element of wanting to play out in court a theatrical piece whose prologue he had written but whose outcome was known only to the Fates. It was a sense, which would undoubtedly have appealed to the one-time Classical scholar, of fulfilling his own destiny, of being both spectator and participant in his own tragedy. He must have been aware that he would have to defend his relationship with Bosie and that Queensberry might point at his public behaviour and his written work, evidence which at worst could only be seen as circumstantial. He cannot, however, have reckoned with the damning evidence which Queensberry's lawyers dragged out of London's homosexual underworld, some of which was disclosed to him as the Marquis's plea of justification a day or two before the trial opened. At that

Lika Joko's theatre critic felt that the first act of *The Importance of Being Earnest* showed promise, the second was ineffective, and the third simply died away. Harry Furniss depicts Oscar personifying his own play.

Mr. O. W. *personifying his own play.*
" *The figure is more than a little weak in the legs.*"

Page from the original four act manuscript of *Earnest*. Ernest's profligacy very much mirrors Wilde's own at the time.

Theatre programme for the first and last performances of *The Importance of Being Earnest*; in the latter Wilde's name has been removed.

St James's Street in 1895 where Wilde spent
much of his time between 1891 and his fall.
An Ideal Husband was written in rented rooms
nearby while Douglas was in Cairo.

Opposite **The Marquis of Queensberry as a recent convert to the new sport of cycling.** From *The Cycling World Illustrated*, 13 May 1896.

point, faced only with a catalogue of 'indecent acts' to answer to, he might have withdrawn, but there, at the end, was *Dorian Gray* described as 'an immoral and obscene work calculated to subvert morality and to encourage unnatural vice'. Mindful that his beloved Flaubert and Baudelaire had been accused in the French courts in almost identical words, was this to be the finale of his own literary crusade against the English? Whatever the truth, 'the lord of language', as he described himself, played that last hand with appallingly high stakes and lost.

Below **The card which Queensberry left at Wilde's club and the cause of Wilde's action for criminal libel, and the envelope into which the Albemarle Club porter put Queensberry's card.**

Once Wilde had instructed his solicitors the Law moved quickly, and on the morning of 3 April 1895 the trial of Wilde v. Queensberry started at the Old Bailey. Edward Carson, a contemporary of Wilde's from his Trinity days, was Queensberry's counsel. To Wilde's delight Carson's cross examination began with his relationship to Douglas. There was no proof and nothing to defend.

He moved on to *Dorian Gray*. Wilde was in his element defending his views on art and morality. Carson quoted *Lippincott's* version, calling the book 'the purged edition', and questioned Wilde about the very sentence which he judged it prudent to omit from the book. 'Have you ever adored a young man madly?' – 'No, not madly; I prefer love – it is a higher form. I have never given adoration to anybody

"Q"

Silhouette of
Queensberry by
Punch cartoonist Phil
May done in 1889.

except myself.' An uncomfortable moment but Wilde was back playing to the gallery. Carson was unable to establish guilt by association. Wilde was full of confidence as the second day started and Carson questioned him on his private life. 'Do you drink champagne yourself?' – 'Yes; iced champagne is a favourite drink of mine – strongly against my doctor's orders.' – 'Never mind your doctor's orders, sir!' – 'I never do.' More questions about Douglas and the servant at his lodgings in Oxford. 'Did you ever kiss him?' – 'Oh dear no. He was a peculiarly plain boy. I pitied him for it.' – 'Was that the reason you did not kiss him?' And before long it was all over. It was not on *Dorian Gray* in the end that they got him; by giving Oscar Wilde a day to defend himself and his art Carson caught him superbly off his guard. One fatal witticism too many and he had talked himself into prison. Wilde, as the prosecutor, withdrew the following day on the advice of his counsel. Queensberry instructed his solicitors to send the files to the Director of Public Prosecutions and Wilde was arrested that evening.

His first trial against the Crown started three weeks later and finished with a hung jury. Released on bail, no London hotel would take him in; Queensberry had seen to that. He eventually took refuge with an old friend, Ada Leverson, and her husband. The matter could have ended there, with Wilde suffi-ciently disgraced in the public eye; the Law was not

Queensberry
caricatured by Spy
(Leslie Ward) in
Vanity Fair, 10
November 1877.
At the time of his
vendetta against
Wilde in 1894–5
he looked just the
same.

Above **Wilde was arrested in the evening of 5 April 1895 at the Cadogan Hotel.** *Illustrated Police Budget* 13 April 1895.

Right **While on remand, the contents of Wilde's home were sold to pay his debts. Included were 2000 books for £130:** '... my library with its collection of presentation volumes from almost every poet of my time; with its beautifully bound editions of my father's and mother's works.'

Opposite **The** *Illustrated Police News* **of 4 May 1895 views the downfall of Wilde reminding readers of his success in America in 1882 and the sheriff's sale.**

bound to continue the prosecution. But it did, and wheeled in none other than the Solicitor-General himself, Sir Frank Lockwood, to conduct the prosecution in the next trial. Edward Carson is said to have appealed to Lockwood to let up on Wilde but received the reply, 'We dare not. People in England and abroad would say that owing to the names mentioned in Queensberry's letters we were forced to abandon it.' Had Queensberry written to Rosebery, threatening to expose him unless he secured Wilde's conviction? We shall probably never know. More to the point was that an election was due and the Government needed to show that it could bite as well as it could bark after the Cleveland Street fiasco. Wilde was convicted of gross indecency on 25 May 1895 and sentenced to two years' hard labour. Constance, who had sent their sons to Switzerland, stayed on to the end, but now she too went abroad.

BY ORDER OF THE SHERIFF.

A.D. 1895.   No. 4907

16, Tite Street, Chelsea.

Catalogue of the Library of

Valuable Books,

Pictures, Portraits of Celebrities, Artistic Society Prints,

HOUSEHOLD FURNITURE

CARLYLE'S WRITING TABLE.

Chippendale and Italian Chairs, Old Persian Carpets and Rugs, Brass Fenders,

Moorish and Oriental Curiosities,

Embroideries, Silver and Plated Articles,

OLD BLUE AND WHITE CHINA,

Moorish Pottery, Handsome Ormolu Clock, and venturous Effects:

Which will be Sold by Auction,

By Mr. BULLOCK,

ON THE PREMISES,

On Wednesday, April 24th, 1895,

AT ONE O'CLOCK.

THE ILLUSTRATED Police News

LAW COURTS AND WEEKLY RECORD

ESTABLISHED 1864.

No. 1628. [REGISTERED FOR CIRCULATION IN THE UNITED KINGDOM AND ABROAD]   SATURDAY, MAY 4, 1895.   Price One Penny.

CLOSING SCENE AT THE OLD BAILEY.

TRIAL OF OSCAR WILDE.

OSCAR WILDE AS A LECTURER 1882 AMERICA.

OSCAR WILDE AS A PRISONER 1895 BOW STREET.

JURY

SALE OF OSCAR WILDE'S EFFECTS

OSCAR WILDE'S HOUSE IN TITE STREET.

Opposite **Wilde imagined in his cell** by the *Illustrated Police Budget* of 20 April 1895. The reality was far worse: no armchair and certainly no newspapers.

Below **Queensberry's fight with his son Percy in Piccadilly on 21 May 1895**. Percy had sided with Bosie against their father and had gone bail for Wilde after his first trial. *Illustrated Police News* 1 June 1895.

The first six months were spent in Pentonville and Wandsworth, before he was transferred to Reading, a traumatic event which took place by public transport and culminated in his being jeered and spat at on the platform at Clapham Junction. Largely in solitary confinement until July the following year, he had no access to books other than those in the prison libraries which, as he said, were mostly third-rate theological works; nor did he have any writing materials. The torture of silence, no stimulating books and no pen and paper must have been intolerable. Fortunately the Chairman of the Prison Commission, sensitive to Wilde's condition, personally saw to it that an exception was made. It was this

dispensation which gave us the most poignant and revealing of all Wilde's works: a long letter from Reading Gaol to Alfred Douglas now known as *De Profundis*. It is difficult to read it without conflicting

Above left *The Illustrated Police Budget* of 1 June 1895. Wilde undergoes the indignity of a prison haircut after his final trial and conviction. Above Right Wilde's cell (C.3.3.) in Reading Gaol to where he was transferred from Wandsworth in November 1895.

Below Prisoners at a letter-writing session in Wandsworth Gaol. Wilde was permitted to write and receive one letter every three months.

The first page of *De Profundis*, the letter Oscar wrote to Bosie from prison early in 1897. He was not allowed to send it but on his release he instructed Robbie Ross to copy it and send the original to Douglas. Ross in fact did the reverse which was fortunate since Douglas, in a rage, destroyed what was sent to him.

Above **Vyvyan in his first summer of exile on the Continent, 1895.** *(Photo E. Potterat, Montreux)*

Below **Cyril aged about twelve in Genoa, 1897. Constance sent photos of the boys to Oscar on his release. 'I have heard from my wife. She sends me photographs of the boys – such lovely little fellows in Eton collars.'** *(Photo Sciutto, Genoa)*

emotions. The compassion for a man of Wilde's sensibilities being broken in prison for what today is not an offence; the astonishment at his arrogance, his ego, the extraordinary projection of himself into the figure of the suffering artist, crucified Christ-like by society; the touches of genuine humility. Above all it is a record of those last two years spent with Douglas before he lost his reason and allowed himself to be used as a pawn in the game between Douglas and Queensberry. 'He once played dice with his father for my life and lost,' as Wilde said later.

On his release he went immediately to Dieppe, determined never to see Bosie again, and started work on *The Ballad of Reading Gaol*, his cry of prison agony. Constance, still in exile with the boys, had been forced to revert to an old family name of Holland to protect them all from the hostility she mistakenly thought she had left behind in England. During Oscar's time in prison she had talked about taking him back, but vacillated on the advice of well-meaning but meddlesome friends. Left to their own devices she and Oscar might have met and passed time together. He desperately wanted to see his children. It might have given him the incentive to remake his ruined life, though it would not have lasted. Constance admitted she could never have given him the intellectual stimulus he craved. The delay was disastrous and weakened Oscar's resolve over Bosie, with whom he spent the autumn in Naples, alienating

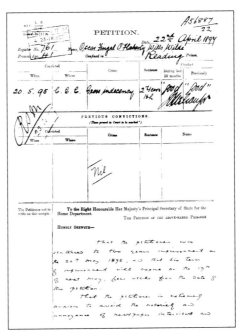

Above **Oscar's mother, who died while he was in prison, 3 February 1896.** She asked to see him on her deathbed but was told it was out of the question. *(Photo C. Chambers)*

Above Right **Wilde's petition to the Home Secretary to be released a week early to avoid the press.** The only compromise allowed was to be transferred from Reading to Pentonville the night before his full sentence was complete.

Right **One of the last photos of Constance who travelled from Genoa to Reading to tell Oscar of his mother's death.** *(Photo by J. Langbein, Heidelberg)*

Above **Ada Leverson**, whom Oscar called the Sphinx. When she met him on his release from prison Oscar remarked, 'Sphinx, how marvellous of you to know exactly the right hat to wear at 7 o'clock in the morning to meet a friend who has been away.'

Below Visiting card case given to Oscar by Ada Leverson together with one of the cards carrying his new pseudonym.

Above **Ernest Dowson**, poet and friend of Wilde from about 1891. They met frequently when Oscar was released and was living near Dieppe.

Mʳ SEBASTIAN MELMOTH

Berneval-sur-Mer, près Dieppe

Oscar Wilde becomes 'Sebastian Melmoth'. He took the name from his great uncle Charles Maturin's gothic novel, *Melmoth the Wanderer*. Pencil sketch by Walter Sickert done in Dieppe, summer 1897.

Oscar and Bosie at lunch in Naples in the autumn of 1897. 'My going back to Bosie was psychologically inevitable. I cannot live without the atmosphere of Love. Of course I shall often be unhappy, but I still love him; the mere fact that he wrecked my life makes me love him.'

Their reunion was a disaster: 'It is the most bitter experience of a bitter life. It is a blow quite awful and paralysing but it had to come and I know it is better that I should never see him again. I don't want to. He fills me with horror,' Oscar wrote six months later to Robbie Ross.

Robert Ross (left) and Reggie Turner who were with Oscar when he died. Turner endured a terrible three weeks watching him deteriorate daily.

Right **Shame and anonymity to the end;** his name was deemed unfit to appear on his greatest comedy when it was first published in 1899. This copy was inscribed to his friend, Robert Ross. George Alexander bought the rights to the play when Wilde was declared bankrupt in prison, and, although unable to stage it for some years, generously paid Oscar money while he was hard up after his release.

family and friends alike. His wife was furious and temporarily stopped paying the £150 a year which she allowed him. He never saw his family again. Constance spent one last holiday with her sons, that summer of Oscar's release, in the Black Forest, before she returned to Italy and they to their separate schools in Heidelberg and Monaco. Six months later she died after an operation on her spine and with her death the door to his children was closed forever. His suggestion to their guardian that he might write letters to them to be opened when they came of age met with an outright refusal.

With little left to live for, Oscar's last two and a half years were a long slide to the grave. He spent them wandering aimlessly around Europe, poor but not penniless, alone but not without friends. 'Like dear St Francis of Assisi,' he said, 'I am wedded to

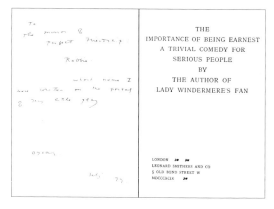

WIFE OF OSCAR WILDE

HERE RESTS IN PEACE
CONSTANCE MARY
DAUGHTER OF HORACE LLOYD Q.C.
BORN JANUARY 2ND 1850 DIED APRIL 7TH 1898

GOD SHALL WIPE AWAY ALL TEARS FROM THEIR EYES.
REV. XXI. V. 4.

Constance's grave in the Staglieno Cemetery at Genoa. Oscar visited it a year after her death. 'It was very tragic seeing her name carved on a tomb – her surname, my name not mentioned of course. I was deeply affected – with a sense, also, of the uselessness of all regrets.' 'Wife of Oscar Wilde' was only added in 1963.

Snapshots taken of Oscar in Rome, probably with his own camera, spring 1900. 'My photographs are now so good that in my moments of mental depression I think that I was intended to be a photographer.' Opposite in the ruins of the Forum. Top Right In front of the equestrian statue of Marcus Aurelius on the Capitoline Hill, Rome, April 1900. Below Left On the steps of St Peter's, Rome.

Above **Leonard Smithers** who brought out *The Ballad* when no other publisher would touch it. A man of louche tastes, he was once described as 'the most learned erotomane in Europe'.

Opposite **Oscar's** writing table in the Hôtel d'Alsace. 'I wrote when I did not know life,' he said to a friend in Paris in 1900. 'Now that I do know the meaning of life, I have no more to write.'

Below **Wilde's** prison cell number appeared instead of his name until the seventh edition of *The Ballad.*

The
Ballad of Reading Gaol
By
C. 3. 3.

Leonard Smithers
Royal Arcade London W
MDCCCXCVIII

Poverty: but in my case the marriage is not a success; I hate the bride that has been given to me. I see no beauty in her hunger and her rags; my thirst is for the beauty of life: my desire for the joy.' Bosie helped with the occasional cash handout; Frank Harris gave him two months on the Riviera in the hope that something of the old brilliance could be rekindled. Oscar tried to write, but the spark had gone. Some anonymous hack work for Parisian newspapers was all he could manage – a poignant contrast to the Oscar who had left Reading determined to make a new life.

His last work, *The Ballad of Reading Gaol,* was published just before Constance's death in 1898. And then – silence. Silence except in pale echoes of the past: a paradox or two; a sudden glimpse of the old Oscar between the lines of the begging letters to friends; a prose poem recounted for a glass of absinthe or a brandy in the cafés of Paris for those who would listen to the talker in exile – a painter of language, a musician of words to the last.

In the autumn of 1900 a recurrent ear infection sustained in prison became serious and needed surgery. Complications ensued and meningitis set in. He was soon confined to bed and delirious, but shortly before the end Robbie Ross fulfilled his last promise to Oscar and fetched a Catholic priest who received him into the Church of Rome and administered Extreme Unction. Oscar Wilde

Left The last bill. The proprietor, Dupoirier, gave him much on credit in the last year and showed him great kindness. His bill was finally paid off by Ross in 1902.

Above Oscar Wilde on his deathbed photographed by his friend Maurice Gilbert. 'The wallpaper and I are fighting a duel to the death,' he remarked shortly before.

Left The Hôtel d'Alsace where Oscar died on 30 November 1900. He lived there for the last year of his life.

186

died on 30 November and was given a pauper's burial in a leased grave outside the walls of Paris. Nine years later, with his bankruptcy paid off by the posthumous sales of his works, Robbie Ross could afford to move him to his present resting place in Père-Lachaise. Robbie's own ashes were placed there at his request in 1950. I am certain Oscar would have approved. 'Friendship', he said, 'is far more tragic than love. It lasts longer.'

Wilde's first grave at Bagneux just outside Paris. His friends could only afford to give him a 'sixth class' burial at the time.

Oscar Wilde's final resting place under Jacob Epstein's monument in Père-Lachaise Cemetery where his remains were transferred in 1909.

Bibliography

Amor, Anne Clark. *Mrs Oscar Wilde: A Woman of Some Importance* (Sidgwick & Jackson, London, 1983)
Careful, well-researched life of Constance Wilde.

Coakley, Davis. *The Importance of Being Irish* (Town House, Dublin, 1994)
Gives Oscar's Irish background the prominence it deserves.

Douglas, Lord Alfred. *Oscar Wilde: A Summing-Up* (Duckworth, London, 1940)
Last and least biased look at Oscar by Bosie.

Ellmann, Richard. *Oscar Wilde* (Hamish Hamilton, London, 1987)
Most comprehensive biography to date but not without errors.

Harris, Frank. *Oscar Wilde: His Life and Confessions* (Harris, New York, 1916)
A colourful, often unreliable, occasionally sensational account by a close friend.

Hart-Davis, Rupert, ed. *The Letters of Oscar Wilde* (Hart-Davis, London, 1962)
Oscar in his own words – the correspondence encyclopaedically annotated.

Hart-Davis, Rupert, ed. *More Letters of Oscar Wilde* (John Murray, London, 1985)
Supplement to the above.

Hyde, H. Montgomery. *The Trials of Oscar Wilde* (William Hodge, London, 1948)
Verbatim account of the three trials.

Kohl, Norbert. *Oscar Wilde: The Works of a Conformist Rebel* (Cambridge University Press, 1989)
In-depth textual criticism by a highly respected scholar.

Melville, Joy. *Mother of Oscar* (John Murray, London, 1994)
Meticulously researched life of 'Speranza' and her influence on her son.

Page, Norman. *An Oscar Wilde Chronology* (Macmillan, London, 1991)
Useful, detailed chronology of Wilde's life in 100 pages.

Pearson, Hesketh. *The Life of Oscar Wilde* (Methuen, London, 1946)
Still one of the best pre-Ellmann biographies.

Raby, Peter. *Oscar Wilde* (Cambridge University Press, 1988)
Concise, very readable insight into the works.

Sherard, Robert Harborough. *The Life of Oscar Wilde* (T. Werner Laurie, London, 1906)
Sherard, Robert Harborough. *The Real Oscar Wilde* (T. Werner Laurie, London, [1917])
Wilde's first biographer and close friend. Full of first-hand anecdotes.

The Complete Works of Oscar Wilde (HarperCollins, Glasgow, 1994)
Most easily available 'complete' Wilde with a selection of journalism lectures etc.

Oscar as seen by Toulouse-Lautrec in the *Revue Blanche* 15 May 1895.

Index

Picture Credits

British Library: 165, 168 top, 169, 170, 171, 172 top right, 173; William Andrews Clark Library, Los Angeles: 7, 35 all, 37, 46, 48, 50, 54, 55 both, 56, 57 all, 76, 87, 95 bottom, 96 top right, 97, 98, 101 all, 102 bottom, 104, 105, 112, 113 bottom, 122 top, 124, 127, 139, 141 middle, 145 both, 146 top right, 148, 150, 151, 156, 158, 159, 175, 178/179, Colour I/8, ColourII/2 bottom; Sheila Colman: 146 top left; Corbis-Bettmann: 64, 67, 84, 85, 92 top, 96 bottom right, 98 bottom left, Colour II/2 top left; Ruth Davis: 130 bottom; Ann Dobbs: Colour I 4/5; The Provost and Fellows of Eton College: 130 top, 131; Mary Evans Picture Library: 162/3, 172 bottom; Harry Ransom Humanities Research Centre, University of Texas: 65, 83, 93 top, 154, Colour I/2 top right, Colour I/3; Hulton Getty: 59 top right/bottom left, 109, 157 bottom right; R.C.C. Hunt: 34; Hunterian Art Gallery, University of Glasgow: 140 top; Christies, London: 44/45, 146 bottom right; Library of Congress: 36 top, 38/39, 66, 68, 69-75, 77-82, 86, 90, 91, 94, 95 top; Magdalen College, Oxford: 36 bottom, 41; Jeremy Mason: 106 bottom, 142 top left, 184 bottom, Colour II/6; National Gallery of Ireland: 18, 111; National Library of Ireland: 12, National Portrait Gallery, London: Colour II/4 top right; Pierpont Morgan Library, New York: 122 bottom; Portora Royal School: 25; Private collections: 6, 32 top, 49, 51, 103, 125, 142 top right, 177, 186 top left, Colour II/4 top left; Public Record Office, London: 164, 175 top right; Robert Robertson: 126 top; Julia Rosenthal: 99 bottom right, 107, 176 bottom; Royal College of Surgeons in Ireland: 11; Nicholas Scheetz: Colour II/5; Collection Sirot-Angel, Paris: 59; Tate Gallery, London: Colour II/2 top right; Trinity College Dublin: 30; Frances Wyndham: 176 top left. All other photographs are from the author's personal collection.